Praise for Talking About Race

Kaolin's narrative is a compelling mix of first-rate analysis, personal stories, and practical, illuminating exercises that help readers utilize this book as a living, evolving document. By asking readers to stop and reflect as they move through the text, Kaolin gives us all a chance to breathe, take in the deep and important material herein, and then push forward in the struggle against racism, in ourselves and society.

Tim Wise
Author, *White Like Me:*
Reflections on Race from a Privileged Son

Kaolin's *Talking About Race: A Workbook About White People Fostering Racial Equality in Their Lives* offers a thoughtful curriculum for white people to do the hard but necessary work of confronting the denial, pain, fear and apathy that comes with growing up in the racist culture of the United States. Drawn from her own extensive life experiences and a course she designed as a returning-to-school undergrad, *Talking About Race* adds to the growing toolbox for anti-racism that helps white people move towards accountability, courage, and freedom.

Mab Segrest
Author, *Memoirs of a Race Traitor*

This is a very difficult topic to explore, study, encourage awareness of, and pay attention to. I find Kaolin's *Talking About Race* a thorough, real, and needed workbook or primer for the rising number of beginning white anti-racists to start or further their journey as they become acquainted with the enormity of racism that persists in the United States. My deep hope is that this book will educate, inspire, and guide a good number of white people who want to organize and build communities to heal our wounded society. Bravo on all the work entailed. I'll be passing it along to people, no doubt about it!

Holly Fulton
Traces of the Trade and "Coming to the Table"

Talking About Race gives a look at the burden whites carry in a racist environment without minimizing what People of Color suffer on a daily basis. This book shines a light on the guilt, shame, fears, challenges and triumphs of unpacking white privilege. I learned a lot. Readers will find the questions and exercises an opportunity to go beyond book knowledge and escape their comfort zone to flex their "racial equality muscles."

Dr. Carlie C. Tartakov, Emerita Professor,
Iowa State University

Talking About Race identifies the onset of racism and will demystify the process of deprogramming (for both blacks and whites). This honest, enjoyable read touched me as a biracial woman, made me laugh out loud, as well as made me hopeful that we are one step closer to becoming "just" different shades of the same human race. Great job!

Carolyn Battle-Cochrane, Director/Producer,
Biracial Not Black Damn It

As a young black athlete growing up in NYC we had to travel to play in white CYO gyms around the city. More times than not, we had to literally defend ourselves against rogue gangs of youths, that wanted to cause us bodily harm as we left the gym. While these experiences helped shape me, I never understood why such racism exists. Kaolin's workbook, *Talking About Race,* answers some of these questions, because now I can hear it from 'the other side.' To hear Caucasian students speak on how they were introduced to racism and their subsequent reaction to it shows us that racism is inherited and not hereditary and can be lessened over generations if properly addressed. I highly recommend this workbook to all seeking to eradicate this disease.

Craig Taylor, CEO & Founder,
http://www.rarehiphop.com

Talking About Race puts anti-racism into action in the classroom. Kaolin moves far beyond mere theoretical musings of white privilege by offering an introspective and applied workbook. This practical book challenges the deafening silence of whiteness and racism that pervades far too many classrooms across the United States.

Jake Alimahomed-Wilson, Asst. Professor of Sociology,
California State University, Long Beach

As a white woman living in New York City, I never thought racism was an issue in my life. *Talking About Race* has redefined the way I interpret the reality of racial equality and makes me see that there is much work to be done, both within the way one chooses (or not) to participate in our communities and our continuing education.

Ms. Kerry K. Dowling, New York City teacher,
Beacon School

Kaolin guides her readers to take a look at their innermost thoughts, feelings and experiences on racism. I realized while reading your book that white people have nowhere to go and no one to turn to when they can't stand being raised with so much hatred of blacks, and people of color in general. I had no idea. I'd never thought of racism that way before. I thank you for this book Kaolin.

Robin Pugh-Perry, Mhs.
http://integraltalk.wordpress.com

This is one of the most revealing and honest books that I have ever had the pleasure to review. I had to read and then reflect, then read some more. *Talking About Race* helps us to splice together our own race stories such that we can understand how history has helped shape this unfortunate racial dynamic as well as learn what we can do to move past this and into a world of racial equality. I think this would be a wonderful educational tool!

Michelle Kaye Malsbury, BSBM, MM
Bookpleasures.com. Also on AmericanChronicles.com

Talking About Race was born from the author's probing leadership and teaching experience. She gives us a vital reflective tool for shifting our latent stereotypical attitudes. The book overflows with sensitive questions and keen observations on a delicate subject. It reminds us that our multiracial culture is a gift, calling us to continually evolve, and widen our cultural consciousness. *Talking About Race* is a unique contribution that touches us all, our past, and our future.

Adele Azar-Rucquoi, author,
Money As Sacrament (Ten Speed Press/Random House)

Kaolin has constructed a powerful tool in the fight for racial justice. *Talking About Race* provides the user with self-help strategies that uproot ingrained prejudices and fosters healing.

Nancy R. Lockhart, M.J.
http://www.nancylockhart.blogspot.com

As an educator who teaches the history of racism, I see firsthand just how much students want to discuss — really discuss — the topic of race. We educators need to do more, and *Talking About Race* is a great resource to get that much-needed discussion going.

Dr. Diane Beers, Author and Professor.
Social Sciences Division, Holyoke Community College

A bold sharing of personal experiences uncovering and confronting racism in the Caucasian world, and a heartfelt meditation on a vital topic, *Talking About Race* will likely push all readers to examine where they stand, and to exercise what Kaolin terms the "racial equality muscle."

Robert M. Wilson, M. Ed., Executive Director,
Veteran's Education Project

My African-American husband and I (myself Caucasian) enthusiastically endorse this book as a tool for helping confront the legacy of racism we all share. This is one of the greatest presentations on the subject of all time!

Elizabeth Merriweather, Co-Founder,
P.R.I.S.M.S. Ministry (Progressive Racial Integration for
Sunday Morning Services)

Talking About Race

Talking About Race

A Workbook About White People Fostering Racial Equality in Their Lives

Kaolin

Crandall, Dostie & Douglass Books, Inc.
Roselle, New Jersey

Published by:
Crandall, Dostie & Douglass Books, Inc.
245 West 4th Avenue, Roselle, NJ 07203-1135
(908) 241-5439
www.cddbooks.com

ISBN-10 1-934390-31-3
ISBN-13 978-1-934390-31-3

Library of Congress Cataloging-in-Publication Data

Kaolin.
 Talking about race : a workbook about white people fostering racial equality in their lives / Kaolin.
     p. cm.
  ISBN 978-1-934390-31-3
 1. Racism. 2. Racism--Problems, exercises, etc. 3. Prejudices--Problems, exercises, etc. I. Title.

       HT1521.K366 2010
       305.80071--dc22

                                        2009043843

This book is dedicated to my son,

Baraka George Williams

CONTENTS

ACKNOWLEDGEMENTS

I am deeply grateful to Jeff Hitchcock for choosing to accept my manuscript and shaping it into the book it has become today. With extreme modesty, you have taught me that less is more. Thank you.

To Elizabeth K. Gordon, a kind and skilled editor, thank you so much for your sensitivity and dignity.

To George A. Williams, thank you for suggesting that I "keep the faith." Today, *Talking About Race* is the fullest expression of that faith in motion.

My daughter's support has always meant a great deal to me. The seeds of her patience and joy about my work have been woven into this book with extreme care. Thank you so much, Amara.

To my aunt and uncle for their love, kindness and generosity, thank you for lifting me up when I was down.

To my siblings and their spouses who helped me muddle through several years of revisions, thank you for each vote of confidence and every single joke.

To my niece Sayeeda who has always encouraged me to write, and my niece Kathleen who affirmed my work again and again with wonderfully cheery emails, thank you.

To my nephew Craig: your smarts, wit, generosity and enthusiasm for my work have touched me deeply. I am forever grateful to you. Thank you.

To my former neighbor, Ann: you opened your heart, mind and soul to me as we both went through a "life review" of some admittedly unpleasant topics. Your enthusiasm for life, your compassion and intent continue to amaze and impress me.

To my neighbor Millie A.: thank you for many a memorable conversation and relief from writing.

To my brother Mr. Paul Graham, Mrs. Ida Williams, Mr. James Williams, Jr. (Champ) and Ms. Marie Sutton ('Rie): you may have passed, but our conversations about race live on. Thank you.

INTRODUCTION

Many people are puzzled by the word "racist" because they are uncertain of its meaning. This uncertainty becomes so unpleasant that when we use the term, we do so with trepidation. We may avoid using it altogether, as if self-censorship will dissolve the power the term has over us. However it still exists and it still has power over us.

Some of you are sorry the term "racist" exists, while others are angry about it. Still others are glad to be referred to as "racist," even proud. If you are sorry about the term, then you already know what the term suggests and you probably believe in racial equality. You may believe that racial inequality is not really something you need to deal with, as if it stands outside of your immediate concerns. Yet when you are called a racist, that personalizes your relationship to racial inequality whether you want it to or not. Being called "racist" may take you by surprise and lead you to be open to the idea that you have always had a personal relationship with racism and racial inequality. It is that real relationship and the myths that have kept us from it that this book talks about.

How and why I created a course titled
Let's Talk about Race

In the fall of 1994 I was a forty-three year old white undergraduate at a university in Massachusetts. While sitting in a cultural anthropology class, I noticed how angry the students were at the African American professor as they learned about racism in class.

Some of the students flat out denied the facts and his right to teach them. Others sat silent and tense, clearly unable to cope with the subject. This professor received hate mail and threats. It occurred to me that the majority of the white students were not simply uninformed about the history racism plays in our culture; they were also passionately defensive while they learned the truth about their own history. I considered their passion a call for help.

We all know that our students may have difficulty with English or math, but they do not threaten the life of the teacher because of it. No one attacks a professor because of the content of their readings or a challenging equation. Students do not insist the facts you present to them are wrong or threaten to kill you because the equation exists! Yet the topic of racism evoked such violent emotions and defenses that I began to consider teaching a course that would assist students in processing racism. I also wanted the course to help them begin to cope with how deeply racism had already impacted their lives. There was no doubt in my mind that racism is an inheritance we must all attend to and even assimilate before we are able to disengage from racist norms and assumptions about ourselves. And that is true whether we are people of color or white. So with the permission of a faculty advisor, I created and taught a course titled, *Let's Talk about Race: Confronting Racism through Education.*

My education

In 1991 I had just relocated from Brooklyn where I had raised my two African-American children in a racially integrated setting. I knew things would be different in central Massachusetts, but I was unprepared for the reactions of the other white students when the professor tried to teach us about racism. The course inspired and directed me, but my education on race is not only the result of academic work.

I began my studies during my earliest childhood when the silence and censorship about racism that so troubled me later in the university classroom prevailed. People of color were in our homes and lives. They were our nannies or maids but never our friends. Their marginal position in white society was tinged with a gnawing sense of secrecy rather than the natural curiosity that created bonds among white people. And there was also great shame, I sensed, connected to the presence of people of color in our lives, shame which, oddly, seemed to bring white people closer together. We never talked about it. Even as a child I wondered why.

While I was in my teens I began to find out. I sought out people of color to befriend. Whites in my life responded with violence. I was thrown out of one home, spat upon, followed and called a "nigger lover." My childhood doctors refused to treat me. Later in college, when I married a black man, the entire neighborhood showed up, as if we were a circus sideshow. High school friends rejected me. One did visit, but only to "see what color the baby was" and turn heel.

I could no longer collude in the silence. I had to speak up about race to protect myself and my two children. No one could do that for me. All the love and support in the world — coming from anyone of color or white family members — could not give me what I needed to fight the hatred that came from my own people. But of course there was not only hatred; there was naiveté about racism, and ignorance, and when there wasn't ignorance there was a very calculated lack of interest in the subject. I had to wonder why. My children were at risk and so was I. So why the apathy?

About my course

While at the university, I was a full-time day student and worked in a residential program for children and adolescents by night. My own children were adults by then, so I had already watched my children move through the educational process. We had been a part of many trends where racism was concerned. But we were never completely satisfied with anything we had experienced. So I decided to write my own proposal and teach a class on the subject. Once accepted, I had a sponsor and went to work.

When I planned to grade the students, one of the department heads exclaimed, "Oh no, how can you grade a course on racism? You can't grade a course on racism!" I was taken aback by her response. The students were writing papers, studying, and participating fully in all the class activities. I knew they would work hard on this subject. However, I conceded to grading on a pass/fail system. The concept was new and needed to be tested. But I am of the opinion that lowering the bar regarding racism in general is not helpful to students. I recommend letting them get full credit for their work on this subject.

I had the privilege of teaching the course for two semesters. I also had the pleasure of having the most amazing students and class participation. You will hear from many of the students throughout this book. The students were of color and European white. They ranged in ages eighteen through twenty-one and came from various states in the USA.

While the course presented many a challenge, the students remain focused, courageous, and willing to reveal the truth of what racism had done to them before they arrived on campus. They also managed to disclose the strains racism imposed upon them once they started college.

They found a voice for a subject in which there was no language before and no one to speak to about it. They came upon and embraced connections to one another they had thought may not be possible. They also showed me that I was right: racism is a burden. Once we identify the source of the burden, we can begin to relieve ourselves of it. But it takes time to do that. It takes strength and risks, courage and clarity. I hope that to this day they are still invested in racial equality.

In this book you will hear from many of the students, with names changed to protect their privacy. They speak eloquently and honestly about stages, dilemmas, and joys we all go through, captured in-depth through dialogue and reflection. I am indebted to them for their active participation.

What educators do not seem to know

My students showed me that racism is a burden. I still find today that the great majority of educators fail to understand that students carry a lot of racist baggage with them from grade to grade in school. You might wonder how I can say that? I can say that because of what I have seen. I have children who went through the school system. I have taught in pre-schools and was a substitute teacher in elementary, middle and high schools. I have worked in a residential treatment center for children and young adults ages seven through twenty-one, and on a daily basis this is what I have observed in our children and adolescents as a result:

- 🍎 Students begin to absorb the racism of others in their childhoods as pre-schoolers.

- 🍎 Students enter elementary schools without sufficient attention given to them for their notions about race and racism.

- 🍎 In middle and high schools, the problem of how one navigates through racism continues.

- 🍎 As a result of the lack of attention on this subject, the isolation and complexity of cross-cultural communication continues to be problematic as our students enter college.

I learned that, regardless of a teacher or residential counselor's desires, racism in these institutions begs for attention, an attention in which employers display no interest. For me, this is clearly another manifestation of the tendency to perpetuate racist norms and assumptions about one another in the workplace. I consider this a tragedy. It is also a problem I wanted to begin to solve. But how? The first step was by making the following determinations:

- 🍎 Students need more support from teachers in coping with the magnitude of the problem of racism in their lives today.

- 🍎 School systems are aware of this problem but do not necessarily know how to correct it.

- 🍎 Schools often lack the funding to pursue their own interest in fostering racial equality in the classroom.

- 🍎 Teachers often struggle with their limitations in incorporating lessons that deal with racism through their curriculum.

- 🍎 When racist messages get carried over from one student to another, other people are often extremely passive in dealing with the situation.

- 🍎 Educators and administrators are afraid to deal with racism in school. Their approach may lead to resentment among parents, who can sue the school and its personnel.

When I designed and taught my course, I felt I was contributing to putting an end to the silence about racism in our children's lives, no matter their age, culture/s or circumstance. I also felt one important and positive coping mechanism is gaining more knowledge of American history and the impact racism has had on our culture. And I felt very strongly that an investigation into the notion of complicity would be a tool in the classroom setting that would assist our students while they make an effort to disengage from racist assumptions about others and themselves.

What did I find? I found that while teaching my course:

- ❦   The students' self-esteem was bolstered.
- ❦   Their coping skills increased.
- ❦   They experience more unity among peers.

I believe that with more classes on this subject, educators in general can walk away from a day's work self-satisfied, assured that the generation of students they are teaching will not be following in someone else's footsteps but have a road to pave of their own instead.

There is a saying regarding education that goes like this: "When you teach, you are preparing your student for their future not your past." It is important that educators, counselors, caregivers and parents keep that in mind. We all know the impact we have upon our youth stays with them for a lifetime. When we manage to strengthen our resolve to foster racial equality in their lives, we also heal ourselves of many of the wounds we have encountered along the way. We, too, deserve the experience of healing from the wound of racism in our lives.

Who should read this book...

Writing a book is very different from teaching a course. The classroom teacher has the opportunity to receive feedback from learners in each and every classroom session. Individual and collective dialogue and interactions become key learning tools for the instructor and student. A book, however, must simply lay everything out at one time, and the author must make her best guess about what the readers will need at each stage of their development.

In this book I have drawn the focus a little closer on white people, per se. This is a book about what white people can do to work for racial equality. But it would be a mistake to say it is a book only intended for white people to read. I hope and believe that the material will prove informative and illuminating to people of color who might want further insight into the psychological and social experiences white people encounter when trying to unlearn the training of a racist society. As a white person, I see distinct similarities as to how European white people experience life because of the privilege and the entitlement given us through the many forms of oppression inflicted upon others. You will read a lot about that in this book.

In the book you will notice, too, that I often refer to people of color rather than specific populations such as Latino/as, Asians, or Native Americans. At the same time, my personal experience has been in the African American community. I believe I only have the right to speak of my own life experience and share what I have learned from it as much as I possibly can.

...and why I wrote it

Because learning how to talk about racism is hard. Most of us "react" to it first. It is a dysfunctional approach, but the best we can do. We are "for" or "against" racism but may not even know what either position actually means to us. The lack of thought that has gone into many white people's position about racism is amazing to me. There is a great and pressing need for materials that intentionally focus on and help white people work on issues of race and privilege. *Talking About Race* tries to meet that need.

Many aspects of the racism I had to cope with growing up seem to have dissolved. Barack Obama is the first black man to be elected President of the USA. These are hopeful times for many of us, but we are hopeful, not delusional. We know racism still exists in this country.

It certainly does.

Regardless of age, status or class, you and the students have something in common. Racism has shaped you. Many of you will be reading this book because you already believe, as I do, that we share a bizarre legacy and you'd like to work your way out if it. Many of us are working on the problem of racism in our lives. We're glad to have you join the effort.

Talking about Race has been written in the hope of encouraging people to talk about what they know. We all know something about racism, don't we? We needn't be historians, journalists, lawyers or scholars in order to discuss what we know about racism. This book encourages you to speak about what you know. It also teaches you how to deal with your newly acquired knowledge within the context of racism, as it enables you to disengage from the power it has over you today.

How to use this book

You will need two tools for this journey: humility and a suspension of judgment. The book asks very personal questions about your own race story and gives you space, in Workbook Writing sections, for your answers. Be sure to give yourself space, too: space to make mistakes, to be uncertain, to have realizations, to grow and to change. Space to accept yourself.

Some of you are reading this book on your own. You want to explore your relationship to racism as an individual. Others will be working in small groups, enhancing your knowledge of yourselves and others on this subject in your effort to do race work in your own communities.

No matter where you are or who is working on this book with you, take steps to assure everyone that what they say is confidential. Trust may take time to build together but mid-way through this book, if trust has not taken root, then you have done something that needs to be corrected. So get some feedback from another race worker and correct it.

If you are working on this book alone in your own home, keep your answers to these questions in a safe space that is for you and you alone. Racism surfaces in the most unsuspecting places in our histories and yet we see it every day. There are contradictions in the process; it does not follow a straight line.

You may even consider yourself a racist and be reading this book for a variety of reasons I am not mentioning here. No matter who you are or what brought you to this book, go through this process as I have asked you to. Answer all of the questions. Don't discuss it with anybody until you are ready to. If you need to change the names of the people you write about, that's fine. All the names I use have been changed to protect people's privacy.

Talking About Race consists of seven chapters. Each chapter includes one or more sets of Workbook Writing questions which draw you into the conversation that began with the class. The chapters work best if read in order, especially the first four. Chapters one and three introduce ideas that chapters two and four illustrate, respectively, with real-life cases. Chapters five and six stand alone a little better and, really, you can read any chapter alone with help from the glossary at the back of the book.

The first two chapters, "Recognizing Racism" and "Resisting Racism," introduce key concepts while giving you the chance to begin to write your own race story. Chapter one explains how racism is intertwined with family life, while chapter two gives an example from the class of a student who came to recognize her father's racism. We look at how Claire reacted and talk about what else she might have done.

Chapter three outlines common defenses and insecurities that stop us from seeing and working on racism, with ways around those obstacles. In chapter four, we discuss the thinking of a student to help us understand and take responsibility for white privilege. The chapter ends with an assigned outing to an integrated place that should really open your eyes. That's followed by a between-chapter Workbook Writing Interval. This section is made up of reflection-provoking questions that let you pause and consolidate what you have learned in the first four chapters, and prepare you for the leap into the new identity covered in the last three.

A word of advice: keep all your workbook writing. When we approach racism consciously and voluntarily, the discoveries flow fast. We hear and see everything differently. We become keen observers of people and society. We also become more self-aware and realize that we have many choices about how to navigate through racism. You will know a lot more about yourself when you finish this book. Your answers matter. Keep your work.

After the writing interval, we begin to reap the benefits of our work as we discuss and develop a new racial identity in chapter five. We read about Maria, still struggling to make sense of what happened around her high school prom. We read about racial maturity, and reach for it. In chapter six, we begin to glimpse what racial equality would look like and the concrete steps we can take to make that vision a reality. We read about Roger and William, two friends pulled over for "DWBW" — driving while black and white. You get to apply what you have learned in the previous chapter to an analysis of their complicated situation.

The final chapter employs a metaphor to help us understand just how surrounded we were by racism growing up and yet how uncomfortable we were with it. We always knew we didn't belong in it, didn't we? But how could we get to the place where we belonged? Reading this book, doing the workbook writings, pushing ourselves to enter integrated conversations and places, we have by chapter seven traveled pretty far. At the end, we validate our work and the work of others. We define racism for ourselves. We realize how much we have changed and look ahead to some of the bumps that will probably come in the road, so that we can be ready for them. We know we're not done, or perfect, but we also know that we're not going to be one of the silent ones. We can talk about race, and we will.

Chapter One

RECOGNIZING RACISM

As I grew older I realized that my grandmother,
as much as I love her, was a racist.
Being confronted with such ignorance
from someone you love so dearly
is very hard.

My family will not like that I am changing.
I don't know how I can let them know yet.

Before I knew anything about the history of racism, it was all around me. I slept in it. I bathed in it. I learned how to walk and talk in it. With all of this learning and doing and being in racism, I began to wonder why white people relied upon hating a group of people at all. Their hatred seemed to indicate a greater insecurity. What was it? Where did it begin? Was it in me at birth or would I "catch" it later like the measles or the flu?

Racism was first introduced to me within my family of origin, which remained racist as I grew up. That racism was reinforced by the values in our community, schools and church. At the age of nineteen, I met and married a black man and we had two children. Writing became a coping mechanism. I began to record the daily racist incidents I observed and experienced. The journey I have been on is also your journey, and the journey you are on is my journey. Racism has bound us together, and I am convinced that we will only set ourselves free of it together. Sharing each others' stories is one way to get freer, sooner.

This book tells you a little bit about my **race story.** No matter how old we are, how much wealth we have or don't have, where we grew up or where we live now, we all have a race story of our own. We need to look at our history to examine how and why the roots of racism grew so deeply in our lives. We need to tell our race stories.

In this book you will see how my students lived through their experiences with racism and you will find bits and pieces of your own race story in here. You will also be asked to answer questions, reflect on what you have read, and begin to record your story.

What we already know

Let's take a look at what many of us know about racism, the racism we have been subjected to and the racism we may have participated in.

Racism is not an invisible entity, is it? All we need to do is walk down the street, read a newspaper, log onto a website, or watch TV and we see racism all around us. Racism is in our families, in our communities and in our institutions. You see it in magazines and comic books. It's in our video games and our military. You experience racism in your place of business and you hear it on the radio. You will experience pain as you come to see racism and struggle with its implications, but you have a right and a responsibility to encourage **racial equality** in your life.

Many of you are concerned about the racism you see in your own families. Others have vivid memories of being raised with racism. And still others who are reading this book right now are in a great deal of conflict because they have come to learn their partners, employers, employees, teachers and doctors are racists.

There is a painful awakening we experience as we see how deeply racism permeates our lives. Disturbed, we wonder *What can I do about it? Where do I begin?* When we see it in ourselves we can easily become frightened of it and feel powerless to do anything about it. After all, where has it come from? How has racism crept inside of us? Those concerns are common among white people and they will be addressed in this book.

While racism is very visible, our reactions to it may sometimes be, or feel, invisible, because of **denial.** Yet denial that racism exists does not protect us from it. In this book you will begin to examine what that mysterious something is about racism which causes an uncomfortable stir inside of you whenever anyone calls you or someone close to you a "racist."

We go through many stages, many ups and downs, as we process what we know about racism and move toward racial equality. There are seven principles that may help you make sense of your reactions.

1. We are afraid of racism and its power over us and other people.

2. We are used to trying to conceal our problems with racism from one another.

3. Working on racism may give fleeting results.

4. When we begin to experience unity across racial lines, it frightens us but we are not sure why it frightens us.

5. We fear that our sense of self-preservation dissolves as we work toward racial equality. We wonder what would take its place.

6. We wonder about being disloyal to other white people if we pursue racial equality.

7. The more we care about racism, the more we worry about what it may cost us.

These principals gradually emerged as the students in the course that inspired this book began to express their concerns about racism.

The students' concerns

My students were concerned about how to fight **racist assumptions** within themselves. They also wanted to learn how to confront others when presented with their racism.

One student — I'll call her "Clarissa" — was raised by a wealthy family in Texas. Clarissa, a white student, was a senior when she took my class. She said that she hoped to go to that "unreachable place within myself to sort out and find the origins of prejudice and fear of others I experience now." Her participation in class was so powerful. She loved her family as all the students loved their families. A few weeks into the course she asked, "How will I be able to integrate my family into my life as I do this work?"

Iris, hoped to "gain a better understanding of why people act the way they do in situations regarding the differences between us," as she put it, "racially-speaking." Iris identified herself as Afro-Fem-Centric and believed that "if enough analyzing and effort is put into everything you do, many people will walk away from conversations about racism with different perspectives on diversity and culture."

Another student of color expressed a concern "about the use of the word 'light' in literature and in spiritual contexts. Like 'I saw the light', or 'He went in to the light.' I cannot help but wonder if the 'light' references are simply reinforcing that darkness and even blackness is bad. . . . This really frightens me because it has to be impacting us — all of us."

Asa was a freshman from Brooklyn, New York, and a white student. He said he knew he had questions he had not yet formulated in his own mind but was looking forward to doing that in class. Mari, a South Asian student from a suburb in Boston, observed that "somehow we are strengthened by societal **stereotypes.** They aren't some formless thing that just happens to us. We must dissect them and get rid of them. If we don't then there is no hope."

Jane, a student of color, told us about her history class, where she was reprimanded and spoken to like a child when she brought up anything to do with racial politics. "The questions I'd like to raise in class are simply not welcome," she explained. "As a result I cannot put myself into the class at all. Instead I am on the sidelines." Jane added that while she can cope with this treatment, it is "a shame." She loves history and would like to be fully present in the class. No white student had spoken up in class or approached Jane to acknowledge the problem.

Another student, Amear, noted that "Even when white people seem okay about prejudice, they raise their voice when they speak to me. I am black; I am not hard of hearing. In addition, it happens at bus stops, in stores and in class. This makes me wonder how deep this problem really does go."

As you can see, the students brought many different concerns into the classroom and a willingness to go deep to solve the problem of racism in their lives. One concern they seemed to share was a fear of surrendering to peer pressure when it came to racism. "I often feel powerless and frustrated," wrote Michelle. "I feel unable to make myself heard and am wary of all confrontation." And another student found that whenever she tried to talk about race, everyone seemed to be prone toward "anger or intolerance." And yet she felt the need to push through because, as she wrote, "if I can't share my concerns with others then I feel like a part of myself is being cut off from them too."

Some of us have felt the same way. What an enormous burden our youth have taken with them from class to class, year after year. We all need a safe space where we can begin to talk about that burden.

Racism is our inheritance. We are born into a legacy of racism. A road was paved for white people on the backs of people of color. But many white people have been told that racism is simply not a problem we need to concern ourselves with. We did not begin it, we're told, so why should we be held accountable for it? Exploring black culture is just too complicated for us. Our lives and our tasks were supposed to be simpler. The whole idea of racism, in fact, was to put us in a place that was supposed to be less complicated than the place people of color are put in. So why ask for trouble? Why turn off the smooth, paved road onto rough terrain?

Those who make these arguments know that once we start doing the work we will come to distrust them and question their motives. So the more you do to get involved, the more warnings you will receive about how dangerous it is to get involved.

Racism is an unpleasant topic. Perhaps it is too unpleasant for you. It can get ugly and may be too ugly for you. Our involvement in our culture and its racism is messy. The confusion and mixed feelings we have regarding the steps we take to develop and mature in this work about racial injustice are to be expected.

Disclosure leads us to disruption

If you choose to delve more deeply into racism, you may find that some of the warnings not to go on are warranted. You may find that racism is surprisingly complicated to disassemble. That is true because the healing process from racism depends upon **disclosure** — exposing secrets, myths and lies — and disclosure is usually disruptive.

To handle that disruption when it comes up in reading this book and in your life, concentrate on the liberation from fear and **guilt** that you will experience as you begin the work. Let yourself imagine a life with racial equality. You will then be better able to weather the disruption that comes with disclosure. Or even invite it! How? By keeping your eyes open, by staying awake and staying put when you'd rather run away.

How do you know whether or not you are a racist?

When you have made the decision to leave the subject alone, you have become a racist. You have accepted the lie that the old phrase "the race problem" means "the unsolvable problem" and "the problem that is not my problem." We may be overwhelmed by the first conflicts we feel about racism because we have been conditioned by this lie. Conditioning is unconscious but reversible. How do we begin to reverse it? By realizing that this conditioning is part of our inheritance as white people. So, since the problem is ours, we need to learn how to recognize racists.

Recognizing racists

- ❦ Racists believe they are endowed with certain privileges because they are superior to people of color.

- ❦ Racists believe they need not change.

- ❦ Racists believe the world need not change.

- ❦ Racists want to influence the opinions of others regarding the notion of racial inferiority in people of color.

- ❦ Racists reinforce racial stereotypes whenever they can.

Many of us with the best intentions become racists very easily with almost no knowledge of how this transition took place. The transition began very early and subtly when we first accepted the perks and benefits that come with being white, known as **white privilege** (more about that in chapter four). These perks guarantee us free membership in the majority, or **inclusion.** When we begin to let that go, or even to think about letting it go, we experience rejection and loss: exclusion. We don't want to leave our special status behind; we don't want to be left out.

When we decide we can't sacrifice inclusion for the racial equality we claim to believe in, we experience conflict, resentment and anger. Failing to cope with these feelings, we wait for **apathy** to kick in, and it often does. How do you know you have become a racist?

When you give in to apathy and accept the racist norms around you, you have become a racist.

But you had "help." Let's look at where it all started.

We begin to experience racism
when we are young

When asked "What is your first memory of color impacting your relationships?" my students responded with very early memories. Here is what Ellen remembered. She was white, Irish, and came from the South side of Boston:

> I remember as a young girl visiting my grandmother. I would hear her refer to black people as "niggers" and "those colored people." I did not know what those names meant. I only knew from the tone of my grandmother's voice and the look on her face that they were bad. It seemed that whenever she would sit down and watch the news, she would comment on all of the crimes and problems in the nation, attributing it to those blacks. This left me feeling very confused. How could it be these people whose only difference between us was their skin color were responsible for such bad things? As I grew older I realized that my grandmother, as much as I loved her, was a racist. Being confronted with such ignorance from someone you love so dearly is very hard.

Tony, an Italian and raised in New Jersey, had probably already learned a similar lesson in his family by the time his sixth-grade peers gave him this review:

> The grammar school I attended was primarily white. I will never forget the first time a black student entered our small sixth grade class of thirty-two. The girl's name was Jan. I remembered we shared the same birthday and I greeted her as I would any new student. We played together at recess, where I introduced her to my other friends. I noticed that just because of the color of her skin people acted strangely towards Jan. The girls were frosty to her while the boys just teased her outright.

And a third white student, Maria, told of coloring at a birthday party that included a girl of color. When the girl asked for a brown crayon, Maria recalled,

> The mother of the child whose birthday it was seemed irritated by that request, and she said 'No. We throw out the black and brown crayons when we get them because they are dirty' . . . . The girl withdrew and seemed scared. Now I am surprised she even stayed but she probably had no choice.

Racism enters our lives when we are young and dependent upon others. Is it any wonder that as adults we often feel powerless to do anything about it? But we are not powerless. Just recognizing and accepting the fact that we were born into this dilemma empowers us. We can choose to align ourselves for racism or against it.

How do we align ourselves against it? First of all, be aware of what keeps us aligned with it. We may try to defend racism in order to protect our attachment to other white people. We're desperately trying to preserve that sense of inclusion, belonging, unity, our very identity! And yet we know something is wrong. It's as if we're trying to lie down and get comfortable in a bed of thorn bushes. It's not working, and the conflict seems to follow us wherever we go. We just don't want to see the people we love within the context of racism. We want to grow. We don't want to be racists, yet we don't know how to cope with the people in our lives who are.

We learn to feel helpless about race

There is a **learned helplessness** that we often surrender to when the issue is racism. I believe many white people are afraid to care about race and racism because of this. Family, teachers, friends, and society in general taught us that we must learn to live with racism because conflicts over race can never be resolved. For many, this learning may come so early they don't remember it or notice when it is being reinforced as they grow up.

One of the students did notice helplessness being taught in her high school and later on the college campus:

> When there is a conflict between a white person and a student of color, there is never a mutual conclusion drawn about it. Teachers remain silent. They never get involved or seem to care. But when there are other issues among students they do something. They try to mend the conflict. Now it seems that we become what we have been exposed to, as you said in class, that 'learned helplessness.' I am very scared of that now because I am more and more aware of it.

Learned helplessness taught white people that we could do nothing to solve the problem of racism in our lives. But white people are not helpless. We have a frightening position of power over racism, a power that is in fact a continued consequence of racism. We must use this power to look honestly at how we lived with racism all around us while doing nothing about it. We must fight for the kernel of wholeness and integration we seek.

Now it's time to begin. This is a workbook, after all. Please take some time to reflect and write your answers to the questions on page 21.

The things we do for love

When we question racial inequality, our families and communities respond with fear in their faces, anger in their eyes, and disappointment in us. They want us to follow in their footsteps, and we want to continue to believe they are people worth following. But what happens when we figure out where their path leads?

Wrote one student,

> I wanted to continue to have faith in my aunts and my mother. To convince myself they did not mean to use racist language. . . . But my heart sank and I couldn't do that. I felt ashamed of them. As if their racism would naturally rub off on me. As if there'd be nothing I could do about it. It is so painful and confusing separating yourself from it in your own family. And you never see them as you once did. You lose a part of your love for them, safety and especially pride.

WORKBOOK WRITING 1-a

Think about the first time you heard a racist word or phrase and answer the following questions:

1. Where were you at the time? Who was present?

2. How did you feel immediately afterwards?

3. What did you do about what you felt?

4. Should a person of color hate white people?

5. Can a person of color trust white people?

6. Now, think about the first time you felt a racist assumption. What did you assume?

7. Do you remember learning that assumption? If so, when, how, from whom?

Before we turn twelve, many white people experience a **quagmire of conflict.** We step into it with our first questions about our value versus a person of color's. We see how our elders and teachers struggle to explain racial inequality. We sense insincerity, a disconnect, fear, and evasion. By questioning inequality at all, we begin to lose the foundation of innocence on which racism's whole house of cards is built. The adults in our lives see this as a sign that they have failed us, for much time, energy and money has been invested in our blind acceptance of the racism in our lives.

When our loyalty to loved ones is at issue, we may sacrifice our desire for racial equality. It is easy to give up, easy to give in. We don't like to accept the challenge of change or take on the risk and consequence of loss. We'd rather many people continue to suffer than to have one person in our family suffer because of our beliefs or desire for racial equality.

To "protect" each other we protect racism

The quagmire of conflict includes a real fear that if we resist racism we may put our loved ones at risk. What might happen?

- ❦ Neighbors might lose respect for us.
- ❦ If neighbors look at us critically, they might see other things about us that they don't like and which we would then feel ashamed of.
- ❦ If the community rejects us, we will lose our status and privileges.

We need inclusion in our families and communities. Many believe they cannot live without it. It may seem that we can secure that inclusion only through sharing racism. It's how we show support to those who have cared for us.

This quagmire of conflict contributes to many dysfunctional aspects of white family life. If our love for one another depends upon the certainty that we will accept the stranglehold white supremacy has on our most intimate relationships, then we cannot be surprised at the extent to which mental illness, alcoholism, and drug addiction take over and destroy us. It is like trying to keep a volcano from erupting. Sooner or later something is bound to explode.

We cannot move forward on racism without looking back at our childhoods and recognizing the quagmire of conflict we lived with. If we refuse to look back, making the whole issue taboo, then we will probably be strongly motivated to keep others marginalized, segregated, in their places. If they – African Americans – are out of sight (we may feel), then we are safe from that upsetting quagmire of conflict.

But gated minds lead to gated communities. And racism is sustained. Recognizing this is part of recognizing racism.

Your race story

Now that you have begun to recognize racism and its origins, you can begin to discover your own unique race story. We each have one. And we will each write about it. But how do we begin to tap into it? We begin by reflecting on how we have formed our ideas about race.

The positions we have held about racism can change and we can grow. How? By making connections between our past and present. It is important to see how our point of view about racism has been shaped by others. We have not drawn certain assumptions about ourselves or anyone else alone. We are the product of many other influences and so is our understanding of others.

On the first day of class I asked the students to answer a few questions that I want you to answer too. There is no need to rush and no one is looking over your shoulder.

I have chosen these specific questions because so many people I have known have vivid memories of how racism was first introduced into their lives. So take your time and be honest and try to answer all of the questions before moving ahead in the book. You will be surprised at how much your answers have continued to have an impact upon you and your own race story.

Expect these questions to be difficult to answer and just as difficult to write about. But working toward racial equality is work. If my students could do it, then you can too!

My students got very quiet when I asked them to think these questions over. It was not easy to bring their aunts, uncles, grade

,

1. When was the exact moment when your opinion of someone became a prejudice against them?

2. When did you gain approval from someone because of your anger at a culture?

3. How old were you when violent reactions to any ethnic group were acceptable in your upbringing, in or outside of your home?

4. In a classroom, has a teacher ever offended you because of your ethnicity?

5. On your first job, did you ever treat anyone with extreme prejudice?

6. Were you ever ridiculed or assaulted because of your opinion about racial equality?

school friends, teachers or ministers into class but that is exactly what they had to do.

We often hesitate when we are about to speak in public of the people we love or trust. After all, they are still people we rely upon and they upon us. And it is even harder when the subject is racism because we all have at least one person in our family who is, let's face it, a racist. Many of the students' own parents were putting them through school. How could they possibly speak of their parents as racists among a classroom of diverse students? How could they dare to speak out elements of racial discourse that might offend the student sitting next to them?

But they did dare to speak out. I ask as much of you.

Exercising the racial equality muscle

As you begin to tell your own race story, to relinquish the privilege of ignoring the problem of racism in our lives, and start to think about how your family shaped your ideas about race and how loyalty and fear may hold you back, you are beginning to develop what I call the **racial equality muscle**. Here are a few intentional things that I want you to do every day to strengthen that muscle. For faster progress, keep a daily journal with your observations in it.

- ❦ Notice the people you speak to and who speak to you. What kind of interactions are you having? Do any include concerns about safety? Are they affected by racism?

- ❦ Are you willing or able to discuss racism in your own home? At work or at your church? If not, what's in the way?

- ❦ When you see racism, do you ever step in and say anything about it?

- ❦ Can you bring up topics in this book with your neighbors?

We can stray from the comfort zone

You needn't be discouraged by what you have read. You are doing something right now that can and will move you toward the goals you seek and the racial equality you would like to foster in your life. Continue to read this book and do the exercises in it. Few of us would argue that white people are safer than people of color. Few of us would argue that white people are not given an advantage over people of color. Right now you are doing one of the most difficult things one can do about racism: You are looking within. You are breaking it down, considering your options, learning to recognize racism and dealing with being white. You are stepping out of your **comfort zone.**

There is a great fear tied to this work which you will be untying in order to find out who you really are, what you can really do, and who you can really become. You will learn how to stand up for yourself and accept change, a worthy sacrifice, as you move from recognizing to resisting racism.

CHAPTER TWO

RESISTING RACISM

I fell back on my big, white, fluffy bedspread and stared
at the ceiling. "Is this my family? Who am I?
Am I a part of them? How can I be?
How can I live with them, look at them?
How can I stand myself?"

Celebrities and all they represent can touch a part of us that unveils our truest feelings about race – feelings and opinions that might otherwise remain masked. One of my students, Claire, discovered this when she heard her father and her brother talking about a well known African American singer. Her father's true view, once revealed, disrupted her ideas about her family and herself. She hid away for awhile, caught in the quagmire of conflict discussed in the previous chapter. During our class, though, she surfaced, ready to dissect the incident as part of her own race story. It was a story, she realized, with larger patterns the rest of the class could relate to and learn from.

From the very first day of the semester, Claire was forthcoming about her concerns. She lived in a mostly white town with a small but growing black population. Along with the growth in the number of people of color came an increase in racial incidents from the white population. After several such incidents near her home, Claire came to believe that many of the white people in her town were racists. Having several friends of color, she was determined not to let peer pressure affect her. But her friends of color had gone away to college, just as she had. The pressure was on.

Claire lived in a single-parent household, her mother having died a few years before. Her parents had raised her and her older brother to believe that all people are equal. That made the conversation described below all the more upsetting to her. When it happened, she was sitting in the living room after dinner watching TV with her father and brother. Her father was surfing the channels when her brother cried out for him to stop and go back. A popular black female singer was on. We'll refer to the singer as "Paige Clark."

Claire remembers the conversation:

"Paige Clark, she's a goddess!' sighed my brother.

"Who's that?" my father asked.

"Paige Clark ... she's a singer and a goddess."

"She really is attractive for a Black woman ... Ted, would you marry a Black woman if she was beautiful?"

"I'd marry a Black woman if I loved her, whatever she looked like."

I felt so proud to hear my brother say this. I always saw him as a big, dumb jock even though he's seven years older than me and in college. I like to think I'm the sensitive, intelligent child.

"You wouldn't really marry a Black woman, would you?"

"Well, it doesn't seem very likely, but I can't say I wouldn't."

"Are you trying to piss me off?" My fathers' tone had changed. I slowly looked over at him, and he was sitting up straight and visibly angry.

"I piss you off? Nah, I'm not trying to do anything, we're just talking."

"Well, I just want you to know where I stand. You marry a nigger and you're no son of mine, do you understand? You won't be welcome in my home!"

I stared at my father, "Dad ... you are joking?"

"I'm not talking to you, I'm talking to your brother ... Mark, did you hear what I said?"

"Yeah, whatever dad, forget it."

Then my brother turned toward the TV and started watching the basketball game. My father settled down and watched the game too.

I sat stunned, looking at my father and brother in disbelief. What's going on? Is dad drunk? Dad has black friends at work ... they have been over to our house in the summer. Why did he say that? My parents always taught me all people are equal. Was it a lie? I don't understand he's watching TV like nothing happened.

I had to get out of the room. I got up to go, a little afraid my father would ask me why I was leaving ... what would I say to him? I locked my bedroom door and turned on the stereo. I fell back on my big, white, fluffy bedspread and stared at the ceiling. Is this my family? Who am I? Am I a part of them? How can I be? How can I live with them, look at them? How can I stand myself?

Claire's struggle to come to grips with the attitude of this man she loved and needed was sad but not very surprising. Lots of us have gone through this at home. In my analysis, which I shared with Claire, can be seen a common pattern that is worth analyzing in detail.

A 13-step analysis of Claire's Story

1. "I stared." (The ever-popular gaze at the offender.)

2. "You must be joking." (No one means what he or she says when they are being a racist; he must be kidding.)

3. "Yeah, whatever dad, forget it." (Your brother is discouraged if not altogether defeated.)

4. "Stunned." (The eternal **freeze** when undeniably confronted by racism within the family.)

5. "Disbelief." (Denial often suppressed; or inverted anger as you get a glimpse at the road ahead of you.)

6. Question: "What?" "How? " (Then the obvious contradictions in statements and beliefs about your fam-

ily from past statements that had confused you more than ever about your family and your place within your family.)

7. "Did he lie?" (A lack of trust in Dad now.)

8. "Is he drunk?" (He must be anesthetized if he is a racist.)

9. "Got to go." (You must detach yourself and separate from racism/him.)

10. "Fear." (Fear of departure; becoming disengaged; letting go of both trust and faith in Dad and in Mom - regardless of the past history in both relationships.)

11. "Nothing to say?" (Hmm. Not necessarily! But we do remain quiet as there is a lot at stake and much to think over.)

12. "I would rather lock myself up in a room than fight him." (**Disassociate.** Turn on the stereo and drown out this eventful knowledge of self and Dad and the resentment you may feel toward his power, his dominance, and his control over your life.)

13. "How can I stand myself?" (That's a great question. A reassessment of identity of self flows out of you. Questions, questions, questions.)

Claire sensed that she was not alone in her ideas about racial equality. But her brother's seeming surrender and her father's silencing of her made her feel that she was indeed very alone. What would you have done in her shoes?

A consequence of silence is low self-esteem

"How can I stand myself?" Claire asks at the end of her story (which was not the end of her story of course). Many of my white students realized that they had been stuck in the quagmire of conflict over race for years and they were troubled by what they had done and not done. In some cases, the sheer intensity of their conflict left an uneasy presence in their later lives.

| WORKBOOK WRITING 2-a |

If you had been Claire ...

1. Would you have gone into your room?

2. Would you have put on the stereo?

3. Would you have remained in the living room with your father and brother?

4. Would you have argued with your father about racism? If not, why not?

5. Would you have questioned him about his poker buddies who were of color?

6. Would you have asked your brother to leave the TV off? What else would you have done?

WORKBOOK WRITING 2-a

7. Have you ever experienced any of the 13 steps above? If so, which one(s)?

8. Is there a step missing? If so, what is it?

You will meet Marie in chapter five. Marie disclosed her father's racism because she decided to attend the high school prom with her African American friend. When her father forbid her to go she became genuinely confused about the value of a friendship when pitted against the value of her father. Her confusion lasted years and impacted the quality of her future friendships as well as her self-esteem.

Another student, Nell, remembered a conversation with her mother in which her mother clearly expressed racist opinions. Her mother used the word "nigger" and referred to Nell's acquaintances as "them." Nell was upset because her sisters accepted it. She was not sure what to do or how to do it. She was even more disturbed by this because her mom worked for a social services agency. What really challenged Nell was the question of how to perceive her mother. Was her mother good or bad? Was her mother guilty, innocent or naïve? Answers to questions like these must be sorted out in our relationships to our family members if we are to feel good about ourselves.

Claire, Marie and Nell, like many of us, were confused when they recognized racism in their families and feared resisting it. Such fear may lead to a loss of our humanity. We find it easy to give up our dream of racial equality because we developed it much later than our loyalty to our family. In our family, we find a reliable comfort zone.

The comfort zone welcomes you as long as you put your own restlessness about racism aside or suppress it until, out of utter neglect, it withers away. If you can ignore racism, other racists imply, then your ability to deny yourself will be rewarded with comfort. Why leave the comfort zone?

What's remarkable, given the fact that we are trained to believe that people of color have nothing in common with us, is that many of us do try to leave. And we succeed.

Race work requires introspection and action

No one could argue that Claire had a lot to think over and the consequences to her of disagreeing would be severe. Her silence, in some ways, made sense. And yet, sometimes when we engage in introspection that is dependent upon silence and betrayal, we are doomed as a result. When we take a look at Claire's father we see the ideology of oppression, repression, control and violence. He gives his children fractured relationships as a result and they take these fractured relationships, whose origin is racism, with them wherever they go. There is no way Claire's family is not hurting. It is certainly hurting Claire and her brother. It seems to me that situations like these are calling out to us for a massive union and healing.

How much longer can we go on denying that we have been controlled and controlling, conflicted and conflicting? We are almost, if not entirely, as afflicted by the same perversion of power as people of color. When will we give it all up? Many white people want to be part of a truth not a lie. We want to be able to speak about what we know is true about us and we can sacrifice for the honesty we want once we have made the decision to do so.

Who willingly gives up what we have come to believe belongs to us? We do.

Who willingly sets out to repair damage exacted upon others by our own ancestors, uncles, mothers, sons, neighbors and fathers? We do.

The results that come out of working on your relationship to equality often become more engaging, intimate and transforming than you might imagine they could be. Your relationship to equality can and often does become a work-in-progress as it shapes and re-shapes your choices and your freedoms. Only you can explain what the losses you incur may be along the way.

The seven phases of recognition

We undergo seven phases of recognition when we act to resist racism:

1. We must continuously shape and reshape our identity.

2. We experience loneliness.

3. We rely upon others who are resisting racism.

4. We realize that we are not the only one who is in pain, who is overwhelmed by grief or rage when we see our family's and society's duplicity regarding racism.

5. We learn that we are one among many who are grasping for solutions.

6. We gain a keener awareness of the risks we are willing to take.

7. We understand that racism is vile and violent, that it includes a psychic, emotional, spiritual, intellectual, physical and economic attack on people of color.

Racism violates the human rights of people of color and calls for ongoing resistance. The more we know about the subject the better off we are. Take responsibility for yourself. Recognize that living a life that disavows and resists racism may mean that through rejecting inequality as an inevitable part of being white, you are taking responsibility for yourself. By confronting racism, you have begun to put yourself forward in life without taking anything away from someone else. This is the nature of resistance in action.

We are still finding effective ways to resist. Perhaps answers are interchangeable. Maybe every ten years or so they change according to the trends of the times. We know when there are advances made in this area or losses. We know when there is hope about racial equality and when there is not.

So far there is a tug-of-war about it. If racism will ever stop, it will be because of you and what you are doing about it. It will not stop by itself. Overcoming racism needs attention, commitment and action. The condition of racism exists today because there are not enough people doing something about it.

Racial violence

I'd like you to stop and think about racial violence. Do you see a connection between racism and violence? I ask this because some of us have been sheltered from racial violence. We may consider it threatening on some obscure level, and disturbing. Others we know have been exposed to it or even victimized by it, but it is still a bit out of sight for us. Of course there may be some readers who have been responsible for it, although your understanding of your role in a racist encounter may be different today than it was yesterday.

When we watch racial violence on TV we can say it is awful because it looks awful, but we remain safe under the assumption that racial violence exists outside of our lives. We place an invisible barrier called disassociation between what we see on TV and what we experience in our own homes and communities. I have often wondered what actually constitutes racial violence for us. How do we assimilate what we see, hear or listen to without acknowledging our own involuntary immersion within it? What about the threats we have been subjected to, the warnings to remain complicit in racist viewpoints and behaviors? What about the things we are told will be taken away from us if we pursue racial equality? What about the rejection of white people we have already experienced? Some of my students got ridiculed for taking this course. One was made a fool of by her peers. Each time the students showed up for class or talked about it to others outside of class, they took a risk.

Why were they at risk? Because they were stepping outside of the **white box** and working the racial equality muscle. No wonder we can be confused about our role in racism, given the assaults on our character we experience when we are not racists. No wonder we have been isolated and abused in many situations. No wonder we break down, give up, and give in to racist norms and assumptions about ourselves. There is no excuse for us when we look at the lives racism has shaped and destroyed. But there are reasons why we have not sufficiently addressed racism in this country. We have been subjected to many a manipulative tactic designed to keep us in the smaller maze, looking at the smaller picture of family instead of the larger picture of humanity.

In my own experience, dating a black man in college (my future husband) made me a target of racist violence. When my father learned of the relationship he locked me in a room, bolted the windows shut, and held me captive there for days. I was given food on a tray and a pot to use as a toilet. Other families knew what was happening but refused to help, agreeing with my father that they would "go to hell" if they did. Later I was called "nigger lover," visited and threatened by a KKK member, and my husband and I were refused all but the smallest, dingiest places to live with our two small children.

When we study African American history, we study the history of white supremacy and the violence inherent in the behaviors of white people. A natural product of this exploration is the acknowledgement that racism and protection of white privilege is intertwined with the institutions we're part of – our family, schools, work places, economy and government. At the root of this **institutionalized racism** is violence.

WORKBOOK WRITING 2-b

Here are five questions I would like you to answer before you move on to the next chapter.

1. Is a loud disagreement violence?

2. Is being told you will be disowned by your family if you do not remain complicit in your family's racism violence?

3. Is being picked up and arrested in an interracial setting an act of violence?

4. Can extreme passivity be considered violence?

5. Does racial violence wear many masks?

Talking About Race

CHAPTER THREE

DEFENSES AND INSECURITIES

*The more involved I get in this work, the more I can
see why white people don't get involved in it.
There are many risks but most of them are
psychological. At least that is true
for me right now.*

A white student in the class told this story:

> I was in a day care center one day when a little white girl
> aged four or five grew impatient with the black boy she
> was playing with and called him "nigger." The teachers
> in the room stood waiting for the mother to take action.
> The little boy, who was named Nathanial, stared sadly at
> the little girl. The girl's mother appeared a bit flustered,
> but she did not apologize to Nathanial or scold her
> daughter. Instead, she went to the girl, put her hands pro-
> tectively on her shoulders, and said, "Oh, she doesn't
> mean anything. She even dances like a little nigger some-
> times!"

These kinds of exchanges happen often in our schools, at every level. It happens at work and on the street. Many of us have been a part of those moments when we are not quite sure what to do, when we try bringing others in on our racism as if it really is a joke, or some sort of slip. As if it is all "okay." As if we mean "no harm."

But the harm has been done. The joke was not funny. We are not a part of it and do not want to be a part of it. Yet we don't know what to do about the joker or the person who was the brunt of the joke. We are paralyzed by **defenses.** We have too much repairing to do, too much of our own stuff to attend to, to be of any use.

But we keep having these options, don't we? One has to wonder what Nathaniel has? How often have truly innocent children of all ages been surrounded by white people like the mother in the day care center? Children of color know about racism without knowing what to attribute it to long before white people do. When they are not protected from the hostility of racists, they are even more vulnerable. When teens of color are taken by surprise by a cop or a teacher who is racist, they may not know what to do. They often internalize this hostility and take it as a reflection of some kind of inadequacy on their part. And they discover that they are in danger simply by being themselves. How are they supposed to come to terms with that?

This question sobers us as we start to recognize and dismantle our defenses.

Defenses postpone our commitment to racial equality

The lesson that nothing can be done about the problem of racism left white people with a brand new problem: how to live with it. We solved this problem by developing elaborate denial strategies which we rely upon to postpone our commitment to racial equality and to disassociate ourselves from the pain of racism. In chapter two, we saw Claire using some of these defenses.

Defenses are masks that we wear to hide from ourselves and each other the pain and fear around racism. We live under an unspoken contract with other white people that we will never pull their masks off. Some of those masks are disassociation, ignorance and **false innocence,** feel-good guilt, freezing, and anger.

Freezing

Racism, fear and violence are intertwined. People experience a freeze when they have difficulty coping with their confusion and fears about racism. Freezing is a common occurrence in race work and many experience it very young. Remember Tony? When asked about his first memory related to race he recalled Jan, the new girl who was the only child of color in his sixth grade class. It looked like they might become friends. Then the other kids began to shun and torment her. "Suddenly," Tony remembered, "I forgot to speak up." Tony attributed his silence to fear of becoming a victim himself, and to his knowledge that "I could not bring this problem home." But on another level, he may simply have been struck by the freeze.

When we reviewed America's long history of lynching as part of the course, or read shocking stories of gross injustice in the criminal justice system, my students were initially afraid to care, afraid to feel, afraid to cry. Instead they froze.

Freezing and grief

To get around the freeze reaction in class, we tried to open up to what was beneath the fear that causes freezing. Fear often masks grief. Since fear is an emotion that grips you and is also a coping mechanism, it was important that students knew they could feel the loss of the lives they were learning about.

So much loss is connected to racism. We won't be getting back the lives lost because of racism. We will not be repairing the lives of the people of color racism has impacted so deeply through the centuries. Many white people have been raised in a culture that considers the lives of black women and men as having very little value. So it took a while for the white students to experience sadness for the loss of the lives of those who died in such horrible ways under such tragic circumstances, circumstances that ironically were constructed to ensure an improved quality of life for white people.

Coping with grief is one of the most challenging aspects of race work. We have a right to have our sadness exposed to others about this. We have a right to strengthen our equality muscle and learn how to confront others when necessary about our beliefs. Many white people have substituted learned helplessness and freezing for grief. But when we grieve, we care. When we care, we commit. When we commit, we take action.

Disassociation

Recently an acquaintance of mine noticed that her neighbors, who owned a small farm, had black employees working for them. They worked seven days a week, ten hours a day, and never as far as she could see took a lunch break. Instead of thinking something was wrong with her "nice neighbors," as she called them, she focused on what she assumed to be the patience and stamina of the workers. How impressive, she said, that they could work so long and hard in the heat of summer.

We discussed this a bit more, and she eventually recognized that the workers had probably not been the ones to set their hours. If her neighbors had employed her or members of her own family and treated them the same way, she would have interpreted things differently. She and her family are European white.

Among my students were those who remembered times when they had disassociated as a defense against the pain of others and the reality of racism in their lives. One of them, Mark, recalled a community college he had attended with his sister. There were very few faculty or students of color. Eight of the African American and Puerto Rican students lived in a house called "the ABC house," which stood for "A Better Chance." They usually sat at the same lunch table together, and when they did, Mark recalled, other students referred to them as "a gang."

Mark had spoken with the students enough to learn that they came from unsafe neighborhoods in the Bronx, Trenton, Washington D.C., and Brooklyn and liked the college because "they were safer and they never had to worry about being struck by a bullet when they went out at night." But he took no action when they were stereotyped and attacked. In his telling of it, we can see his sadness about his lack of response.

> I heard that recently someone sprayed "NIGGERS GO HOME!" in shaving cream directly in front of their house. ...Since I have been taking the course I realized that neither my sister nor I even thought about what to do about this situation. Now I cannot imagine letting these things continue. When I go home, I am going to the school and asking them to solve some of these problems. I will go with a list of options and solutions. In retrospect, I can hardly believe that we let it all go — as if there was nothing to do about any of it. Moreover, it was so sad. So obvious. I am not sure what is sadder, the way these students are treated or the complete oblivious attitude and helplessness we both felt. If we had taken action then it would have changed the situation these students were dealing with everyday. I am so sorry to see this the way I do now. It is no wonder they only hung out together, what kind of choice did they have? Who cared? But I know I will return and do something when I go back for spring break."

What's sad and obvious is not so obvious and need not be felt at all once we have succeeded in disassociating from the pain of others. To Mark's credit, he used the work we were doing to wake up, re-associate with the real experience of the students of color at his old school, and in that awakened state he could easily think of "a list of options and solutions."

The illusion of color-blindness

There is a great deal of controversy over white people who say, "She is my friend. I don't see her as a black woman. She is colorless to me." Many people refer to being **"color-blind"** as if it certifies them free of prejudice. They claim they do not see or acknowledge the importance of color in their relationships to others at all.

The illusion that we don't see the color of a person of color is a variety of disassociation. It distances us from the person of color's feelings and from our own confusion and fear around race. Why is this illusion an appealing defense? My students spoke of struggling with racism and wondering how they could be aware of it without being biased. "How do I show support and solidarity without seeming to be patronizing?" one student asked. This concern leads even well-intentioned white people to conclude that it is better to be color-blind, that being color blind is less presumptive.

But isn't it natural to have an interest in someone's ethnicity, to acknowledge it, to want to learn more about it? To say one's color or ethnicity doesn't matter is actually offensive to me. Why doesn't it matter? Would you want someone to dismiss or ignore the fact that you are white and Irish, or white and Polish? If enough people do that or refuse to inquire into your ethnicity for fear of offending you, how do you have a shared experience of self, family heritage, and the norms of your own culture? I don't like to think that I am not really seen by people as who I am. I am white. I am Irish. I am fifty-seven years old. Deal with it. Take it or leave it.

We are all a reflection of our culture/s and our ancestry. Our experience of ourselves is influenced by these factors. That is true of all of us. My black friend is my black friend. My white relative is my white relative. My interracial great-nephew is Spanish and black. Why be color-blind? It's counter-productive to need to pretend that our culture and ethnicity are not integral parts of us. I don't leave my race at the door when I go out and neither do you.

Ignorance and false innocence

Too many white people have confused ignorance with innocence. That's a confusion that needs to stop right here. Thanks to the learned helplessness discussed in the first chapter, we may see racism as too huge a problem for any individual to take on. Because there is no immediate or obvious answer to the "race problem," we assume a posture that equates lack of knowledge with innocence. It may be our way of groping toward a solution, but finding solutions takes knowledge. Without sufficient knowledge of the origins of racism, we will lose our way. Lack of knowledge is not innocence; it is simply ignorance.

We may not know what to do with the information we have gathered about racism but that does not mean that we are innocent. It simply means we have not yet figured out what to do. Fortunately, the loss of innocence brings with it a gift: the realization that individual people do have power over this problem. We can come up with the solutions and use our power to solve the problem.

Feel-good guilt

Along with the pose of innocence is a paradoxical need for recognition and reassurance. We want to be told that we are good people when it comes to race. And what do we do to earn the title "good people"? We feel guilty. We say we feel guilty. We admit to owning stock in that notorious corporation – **collective guilt.**

It seems that as white people we have viewed guilt as a natural consequence of racism, instead of as a natural consequence of our apathy about racism. Once guilt is considered a natural consequence of racism, it becomes an odd sort of affirmation, as if the admission alone is a solution to the problem: work done.

But guilt is not a solution to our problem with racism any more than false innocence was. In fact, when the two co-exist in one person, as they often do, they cancel one another out, revealing just how hollow each was. Innocence implies that you have no knowledge of racism. But if you have no knowledge of racism, then why are you jumping up and down on the collective-guilt trampoline?

Guilt makes way for shame

When real knowledge of American history crashed through the façade of innocence, and guilt didn't work any longer as a solution, some of the students in the course felt shame. When we feel shame we are usually sad and quiet. There is no denial. There is no one to blame.

Shame can be a healing agent in race work because we need to feel our way through it. It is not enough to think our way through. We need to do both. This is what made the course unique, complicated and transformative.

My students shared accounts of shame with me and I share them with you because they are part of the rugged terrain we must cross on our way to racial equality.

> I was in a grocery store in an integrated neighborhood. There were as many black people as white. I was uncomfortable and very self-conscious of being white and their being black. I hated that I noticed it and it was an issue for me. I don't know what the discomfort really is for. I know I must be dehumanizing them in some way by reducing them to the color of their skin. I feel ashamed of myself when it happens. I grew up in a white environment, it was all I knew. I am afraid of the blackness of black people. It may be something within myself they are mirroring back to me. . . . It makes me want to throw up.

> I had an argument about abortion with a black woman a while ago. I cannot even remember the details that lead to the argument I ended up having with her. It got heated and she called me a "white bi–h." I was shocked, outraged, hurt and later ashamed. I don't know why I felt so ashamed? I thought to retaliate by answering "you black b—ch" but I did not say it. I was shocked at myself, ashamed and enraged that it had come to this.

> I am ashamed because in one class I am in, I believed a professor of color could not know more about my country than I did.

> I get confused when I know a white person assumes I am a racist. But I have no problem speaking up if they assume other things about me that are also not true. But then I have to wonder, if I can speak out about other things but not about the fact that I am not a racist, does that mean I am? This scares me. Then I do become ashamed of myself.

> Do we, as white people, give up on each other too quickly when the issue is racism? I am afraid that we do. If that is true, I am also ashamed of that.

Shame means we're admitting that we have before us, and in us, a very real and as yet unsolved problem, and that until we find solutions we are a part of that problem. Luckily, shame can be a temporary condition. No need to sign a long term lease! And have you noticed the prize hidden in the box of shame? It is this: the realization that if we, as individuals, bear responsibility for the problem of racism in our lives then we also carry power to work for solutions.

Why deny a problem you can help solve?

Because solutions take work, and sometimes — especially if those we love are safe from direct attack — we'd rather just play.

Anger

People get angry about racism for several reasons. Sometimes it is because we do not want to have to work through it. We can't see why people or events are making it feel like our problem. Anger pushes the problem away. It silences people who may be trying to tell us their stories and so lets us stay ignorant. It attracts other angry people who conspire with us to keep the masks of denial safely on.

A different form of anger that interferes with racial equality work is when we are angry about other issues and use racism to give them a platform. We may not even know about this anger. It may be hidden to us and only surface as anger at people of color or anger over racism.

Just as fear may hide grief, so can anger. We may have suffered a loss that we have not grieved fully and healed from. Anger can be a sign of that. We all have something to be sad about and we all have someone to grieve over. You cannot work the racial equality muscle if you are simply finding a place for your personal anger. Anger can be like an inflatable balloon used for attention on an issue one may not be willing to work through. Anger can get so big and yet it takes the tiniest little prick before it bursts.

We need to choose between reacting to racism we hear about and see, and responding. This is not something everyone is willing to do or mature enough to do. People are used to reacting. Many use anger and rage to bond with their peers.

We must be dissatisfied with racism in order to take the time to deal with it. We must be willing to train our self to examine our motives while we address it. And we must know that our goal is to disengage from the assumed normalcy racism imposes upon us, and the assumed abnormality it has imposed upon others. Just as one works out at home or in a gym, you work on racial equality. It takes time for you to extricate yourself from these challenges. But there is no doubt that you will need to understand the source of your anger so it can be channeled into action. A white person will never be able to be a person of color. But in order to own up to racism and work for racial equality you needn't be. White people need to transform the meaning of whiteness.

Channeling anger into action

You might be wondering how you will live with anger about racism without self-destructing. One of the most promising ways to diffuse your anger is to be among people who feel as strongly as you do about racial equality. If you need to place an ad in the paper about it, then do that. There are support groups for many other subjects and there can be for this too! Go to book signings to see authors who are writing about this work.

One way in which you can assuage your anger is by living up to your own expectations. Anger may be a catalyst for change, but action will lead you to hope. You have every right to hope for racial equality. Keep in mind that anger is not a basis for solidarity but action is. Anger transformed into action is a symptom of hope; anger without action a symbol of defeat.

You are given a choice. Choose hope.

Defend against defenses

My remedy for the defenses that stop us from being able to solve the problem of racism in our lives is to develop the racial equality muscle. We do that by speaking up when we'd rather keep quiet; by seeing and talking about someone's ethnicity even when doing so confuses or scares us; by opening up emotionally when we'd rather shut down; and by exposing ourselves to books, classes, people and groups that keep us honest when it comes to false in-

WORKBOOK WRITING 3-a

1. Is our anger a testimony of hope sometimes? Or, is anger a symbol of defeat? Can it be a bit of both hope and defeat? How so?

2. Do we have a right to try to remain safe?

3. How can we accommodate the anger of people who are marginalized while at the same time trying to make connections with them and reach understandings?

nocence and displaced anger. Attend rallies, write on the subject and join others who share your concerns. You may even want to start your own group to work on the book you are reading today.

Another solution is to be sure you socialize and even work in integrated settings. It can make all the difference. If that's new to you, we'll get some practice soon, in chapter four.

Facing anxieties and insecurities

Although peers may react to you as if you have changed completely, the transformation to racial maturity and a new identity is not instantaneous. You will experience fears, doubts and delays all along the way. Certain things will be very hard to let go. If you know what to expect it may still knock you down, but you can get up and dust yourself off faster. Some of the things you should anticipate are a continuing desire for status; the temptation to give in to apathy; the need for control and, finally; the related need to compete.

The desire for status

Our desire for status often feeds racism. We want to be better than, higher than, smarter than, purer than... and racism supplies the bottom half of that dichotomy. As long as we need status, for whatever reason, racism is attractive. We may be motivated at one level to transform ourselves by doing this work, but at another level we'd secretly like to keep everything just as it is.

The need for status undermines the new identity. So it's important to know just how important status is to you.

The temptation of apathy

Apathy about racial equality work often replaces or preempts curiosity. Instead of assertion and transformation, we rely upon cushions that will not displace us. Racism is a cushion. As long as it is in place we really do not have to do anything to change it. No one is obligated to care and that is one fact we are all aware of. Apathy is easy, and what's easy, let's admit it, is also tempting.

But apathy doesn't really do the job. If we have chosen the cushion, then you might think racism doesn't bother us, but it does anyway. People cringe when they are called a "racist." They jump to their own defense. They convince themselves they are innocent and use that to justify their ignorance. But as we saw in chapter three, innocence and ignorance are worlds apart.

Questioning the imbalance of power between ourselves and people of color, we realize we have been duped into the notion that racism is unmanageable and not our fault. Yet we see evidence of the contrary all around us. One of the coping skills we have created is convincing ourselves we have plenty of time to deal with this. But what are we waiting for?

Perhaps we are waiting for the pain we witness in others to go away, so we can work it out when we are no longer obligated. Maybe it is too painful to see through the eyes of racism and yet when we look at others we see it so clearly we cannot succumb to apathy. Maybe we are afraid to demolish the myths about ourselves. We put it off, fearing that once the dust clears, we may find that we have very little of our old selves left.

Do you believe there has been a delay in solving these problems? Why?

The need for control

In claiming to love ourselves while bonding together through the myth of superiority, white people have developed certain insecurities as a group: fear, guilt, anxiety and shame. We are not entirely able to redirect these, and so they must be controlled. The appearance of being in control, in fact, defines us. It gives us a common identity and gives our communities a semblance of purposefulness.

In a very real sense, this need for control IS who we are. You can see how, even as our new identity takes form, we might cling to the rags of the old. But remember that control is linked to the continuing existence of racism.

The drive to compete

White people were against civil rights because they understood that disassembling white privilege would eventually disrupt their comfort zones and remove assurances that their children's futures would be comfortably laid out for them. In white families, those expectations were not unreasonable. That is why, within many a white household, racial equality and fear may be synonymous.

If there was no disenfranchisement based on color alone, white people would be competing with people they had never competed with before in areas such as access to jobs, education, housing, and health care. White people are supposed to be winners, and we do not give up this notion without a struggle. Where did we get this idea? We got this idea from European culture.

When we discussed competition among white people in class, it seemed students believed that what was missing most among whites was a spiritual identity that was not dependent upon someone else's oppression. One student hoped for "…increased clarity of vision and understanding." Another said we "seemed to have a love of death over life; violence over peace, rape over love and greed over solidarity."

To this list I would add that we have a love of competition over cooperation. While this may come from anxieties and insecurities, it is such a core part of the white personality in our dealings with other white people as well as with people of color that I want to look more closely at it through an experience I had while working on this book.

I am not competing with you

White people's habit of competition is not laid at the door when we work on the racism problem. While writing this book, I met another white woman who is working on racism. She told me about workshops she'd been running in the community and how frustrated she was by the poor attendance. She said she felt defeated. I agreed that it was hard work and started to tell her about this book and the students I'd been privileged to teach.

She interrupted me angrily: "Yes, but you are teaching people who want to be taught!" Her body language got as hard as a rock and she actually glared at me. It took me by surprise and I could see why people were not showing up for her workshops. We were not doing the same kind of work so her hostility really took me by surprise. But it shouldn't have. I have noticed over the years that white-on-white relationships are often competitive.

I pointed out that our conversation on racial equality seemed to be revolving not around either of the populations we were trying to serve, but her. I told her I wasn't competing with her. She became silent. Those words are powerful among white people: "I am not competing with you."

You might want to say it out loud several times a day, then try it outside.

Racism is not a game. There is no winner. Dismantling it is not fun. There is no end to it.

WORKBOOK WRITING 3-b

1. Where do you have a high status? School, work, your family, neighborhood, religious community? Where is your status low?

2. Do you have unearned status in any part of your life? As first-born, for example, or as a grandparent's favorite? Have you every been conflicted about this unearned status? What would you do to keep it? What have you done?

3. When and how did winning first become important to you?

CHAPTER FOUR

RESPONSIBILITY AND WHITE PRIVILEGE

This fear to stand up for oneself and to know your boundaries when someone has threatened you is something I have been dealing with a long time. I see women of color do it often, even with humor. I am so used to seeing this as a lack of survival skills in white women. But now I believe it may be the effect of an abundance of privilege.

Have you ever wondered how one person of color can represent all people of color wherever they go? That has not happened to white people, has it? You are never referred to as the white woman who came into the store to buy juice, the white player who just joined the team, or the white teacher who taught class the other day.

White people tend to retain our individual identities. We can excel without the assumption that we have to bring the rest of us up a notch in class or status. We can take full credit for our accomplishments and carry that independent credit with us wherever we care to go. If we mess up, we do that on our own too. It doesn't reflect on all white people. This is one of the privileges that we enjoy as white people.

People of color do not have this privilege. Divisions have been drawn between us and that dividing took a good deal of violence in the first place. We may experience fear and loss when we contemplate letting go of our privilege in order to build a world where racial equality is the norm.

Tanya's imagined future

Tanya was a student who worked in earnest, just as the others did. She was white and a bit reserved. She believed her whiteness not only gave her certain privileges but would buffer her from integration. She thought that her role would remain intact for good. It might but it might not. It wasn't easy for her to understand that integration and multicultural influences are here to stay. Tanya had this to say about herself and white privilege:

> I feel as an educated, articulate person of privilege, I have a responsibility to do what I can to help ease the racism problem. The black gang member for example is more concerned with survival and not race relations. I think as a future teacher or writer I have an excellent forum for presenting a more realistic portrayal of racism and a positive portrayal of accomplishments of people other than white people.

Tanya has begun to listen to others talk about race. She has also begun to share her own opinions about it in class and to see her position within it all for the first time in her life. As I had mentioned, she is white. She is also self-conscious about the awareness she has of herself regarding her privilege. Tanya did not know enough about gangs to claim to understand what they care about most. She certainly did not know enough about them to speak of their concern for survival to the exclusion of their experience of race relations. Tanya is imagining them based upon the stereotypes she is accustomed to.

This is a leap many of us take in this process. We see our role in racism, we see our white privilege, and often believe we will maintain it even as the new knowledge of ourselves changes us, opening us up to our wounds and our confusion about racism. This happens even when racism bothers us and we believe it is wrong to benefit from it.

In her account, Tanya reminds us that she is in the privileged position. She may feel this position is temporary or that it is dependent upon her racism. Tanya may not be convinced that her status is permanent; however, the more she exposes herself to this subject the more she clings to that privilege. But, at the same time, she is also beginning to observe and wonder about the real people who are disadvantaged because they are of color.

Tanya's gang raises a gang of questions

Tanya's entry raises the following questions: When Tanya examines herself within the context of racism and inequality, why is she referring to gangs at all? Is she feeling threatened by this examination of her privilege? Is she insecure? Guilty? Afraid? Does bringing gangs into the picture make her fantasies about her future look brighter?

Did she mention gangs to provide a contrast to what she hopes her life and her career will become? Or is Tanya bringing up gangs because she is changing and identifying with people of another class and color? Maybe Tanya has found a way to include a marginalized group in her process because she is aligning herself with an aspect of the disenfranchisement she is studying about in class, in preparation for more knowledge and change.

At this point in her comments do you think she may be scared of identifying with the history she has begun to study in class? Are gangs being used as a metaphor to let her fear became a part of her education?

Or are the strengths of the African American people she is learning about in class becoming too much for her? Perhaps she wants to strengthen her perceived weaknesses, and mentioning gangs might be a way of bringing another form of power and even intimidation to the subject as a way of protecting herself.

Has Tanya managed to invade a still sacred place within her by bringing in gangs to contrast her inheritance of privilege and her fantasies about her future?

Does Tanya retain an element of control over the other students and the teacher by seeing herself as a teacher and planning to impart her wisdom in a future classroom rather than continuing to remain a member of the current classroom that is being challenged by talk of racism, talk which may be weakening her opinion of herself?

Challenging white privilege confuses us

Because we examine racism from one perspective does not mean we can assume we are examining it from multiple perspectives. We simply do not have the layers of information and experience about anything but our own position, and that is not enough.

Tanya showed me that she was confused about herself. Given the content of the class so far, she had every reason to be. Her foundation of white privilege was being challenged by history. She equated the racism African Americans face with gangs but she was really speaking of her own fear. Tanya fears her desire for racial equality because she is finding out there is a lot that she does not know. Maybe she does not even know enough about racism to have a right to desire racial equality. She may be disappointed in herself or in the reality of the situation she is in.

Is it possible Tanya has more to consider and more to see about herself and her identity than she may care to know? Yes. In many ways, the real work is just beginning for her.

The more you care, the more you learn about what it can cost you. Tanya began to wonder: How serious is this? What will my interest in this cost me? The danger that concerns her is not necessarily physical danger, but psychic. For instance, what if Tanya is not in the position of teacher or writer someday? What if Tanya has no "excellent forum" with which to present all she would like to present to others while in a power position? Would that be the end of her involvement in incorporating the ideals of today into her future? It seems possible that if her plans go awry then her politics, good intentions, her desire to inform, educate and compensate for the guilt she feels because she is entitled might just fall apart.

Letting go of the fairytale ending, or: If not now, when?

You will notice as you read this book how a realization that occurs in one instant can become the lesson of a lifetime. You may experience deep feelings of loss as you uncover the roots of racism within yourself and what that racism means to others. Sometimes you feel loss in this process and you cannot be sure why or what that loss might mean to you.

Tanya thought she would become "a teacher or a writer" and "present a more realistic portrayal of racism and a positive portrayal of accomplishments of people other than white." This is very nice and a common thread among white people. It is what I refer to as the **fairytale ending**. The fairytale ending is just a more **narcissistic** version of the learned helplessness introduced in chapter one. It says that we might really do something about the racism problem, something truly big and lasting. But not yet. It's a fantasy that makes us the empowered one with gifts and abilities that give us a missionary-like access to desirable strangers.

This way of thinking is a conditioned response to what we have been spoon fed about ourselves. It implies that there is nothing we can do right now, today. It implies that we need a larger, unsuspecting population to present our point of view to, and furthermore that those imaginary people will actually be receptive to our point of view.

But none of that is guaranteed and you may not end up in a position of authority anyway. Often times we want to come out of an experience with all we can gain from having it and yet remain untouched by it, unchanged. But in this work that cannot happen. A radical discontinuity is inevitable, giving us access to living our truth today and everyday no matter what else we do in our lives.

Only Tanya can figure out what she needs to do in the groups she is part of where inequality based on color exists. She needn't wait until she is out of college, or a teacher, or a writer, or anything else. Racism needs to be addressed in a formal setting as much as it needs to be addressed in an informal setting. Change needs to take place in social settings as much as it needs to take place in our most private relationships.

We hope our sense of self will not be challenged

I gave Tanya this response to her entry:

> It seems useful for you to believe your politics will not be compromised and that you may not have to pay a price for disagreeing with others about racism, just as it is useful to see yourself in a role that does not inhibit you but does allow you to teach because you'd like to impart others with your wisdom and your truth. You also want to be able to exhibit your fair mindedness and sensitivity to racial prejudice to help your class so no one is subjected to racism in your classroom.

> Towards the end of the list of your concerns you paused because balancing an adversarial position can be as taxing as it can be exhilarating. You have funneled a sense of outrage and fear and can see that justified anger cannot be removed from racism.

> You are at the center of these realizations in the world you inhabit and yet your fear of what you are finding out is warranted. When a person evaluates oneself within the institutionalized racism, they have inherited they often do begin to look at how others have managed to navigate their way through that which oppresses them as well.

> From what you have told me about yourself you have a limited knowledge of African Americans and a limited knowledge of gangs. I am glad you shared that with me as your knowledge of yourself is what I have asked you to pay attention to and take into consideration in the work you are doing on racism. You have begun to work the racial equality muscle by drawing the analogy you chose, sharing it with me and considering the feedback I am giving you today.

> Now I'd like to take you a step further by having you write me your plans for today and how racial equality plays into those plans.

Tanya had a lot to think about.

As the course continued, I grew to admire her step-by-step process of growth, the manner in which she remained aware of her fears, and how well she integrated the knowledge she gained in class with her own original intent. That intent was to find out how to recognize racism and have that recognition change her. Before the course was over Tanya began an Amnesty International club on campus.

We have come a long way

We have come a long way on our race journey in a short time. How did we do that? We started with what we know:

- ❦ We know we are a part of an imbalance of power and violence that sickens us.

- ❦ We know that we internalize a problem we have been told has nothing to do with us but we have decided it has everything to do with us.

- ❦ We know we have been told we cannot fix it. But we believe we can and will.

- ❦ We know that we are a part of the problem because we benefit from it and we see that scenario played out again and again in our lives.

- ❦ We know we cannot change the color of our skin so we must find other ways to change our lives and people's opinions of us as we work toward racial equality.

White people revisit racist assumptions

Tanya believed that she understood **multiculturalism** better than she had before taking the class and it is possible that she did. But does her knowledge of African American history give her knowledge of black gangs? No. Yet somehow her understanding of gangs has been merged with her understanding of black culture. Even as she gained some racial maturity, she reverted at times to racist assumptions.

As we saw in the previous chapters, we learn these assumptions very early. They have deep roots in our own family dynamics which in turn have deep roots in America's legacy of slavery. We cannot expect to pull these roots up overnight.

Consider how racism and white privilege has already shaped our lives

Acknowledge the extent to which we depend upon people of color and the deprivation racism imposes upon them. Is it a reflection of the inadequacy of our own inner selves as white people? You must wonder. How we view ourselves depends upon the existence of and the continuation of racism.

Take racism and the privileges it gives us away and we would be completely lost.

Now imagine this: In the first twelve years of your life you were considered perfectly normal. Then you meet someone else who for the past twelve years was raised to believe that he/she is not. How do you suppose you would think about yourself in relation to this other person especially over a period of twenty years or so? You would probably see them as less normal than you are. Or as if there was something wrong with them.

For the individual who was not raised with layers of acceptance, privilege and approval you can see the awful impact inequality would have on them. You can also see how it is that disintegration of racism would take time, because this is still the picture of the world that is being presented to us again and again and we do not stop it. We continue to watch programs, read literature and go to movies that promote racism.

A student wrote,

> I know if I was of color today I would have to prove myself wherever I go. But how could I do that? Which part of me would be able to be pulled out for approval? I realized in this class that that would depend upon where I was going, what I was going for and who would be there. I don't think I'd go out much at all, I cannot imagine having to live like that. I'd have to break-rank and allow myself to be hated. I'd have to allow myself to

draw the needed distinctions between me and this
amorphous white and defend, consistently, this position.

Take a look at how important your whiteness is to others

It took many years for me to understand how important my
whiteness was to others. I may have been twenty-six and the
mother of two before I saw the power it had over my relationships.
I spent several more years hoping I was wrong about it because
the essence of white power for its own sake is so perverse that it
is unbelievable to me.

Now I am middle-aged. It has taken me even longer to come
to my own understanding of white power. People of color do not
have the luxury of fifty-plus years to understand it themselves. They
are not observers; they are subjected to it and the difference between our two positions is vast. The filter of racism has penetrated
their psyches long before it does a white persons' psyche and
white people need to pay far more attention than they do to anyone of color who is willing to speak about it.

White people are often misunderstood psychically, spiritually
and morally within their own families and schools when we discuss racism. Whereas people of color have each other to bond with
against the same oppressor, we do not; we are the oppressor. We are
in a white box. We are on the losing side of the argument as there
is no justification for our power and we know it. We cannot be to
each other what we might like to be without feeling complicit or
appearing to be an opponent to whiteness in general when that is
not the case. We are hoping to unite, not affirm disunity, but where
group dynamics regarding racism is concerned, we're almost in-
stinctually pitted against each other.

Can a white person survive without group dynamics validat-
ing their socially constructed superiority?

We may not be able to change the color of our skin in order
to reconcile this problem. We may not be able to rely upon one another either.

Beyond reading and talking

The students' admission that racism exists in many of their relationships was very difficult for them in the beginning of the course. But I did not push them beyond their limits. I let their weekly responses, which had to be at least three pages long, be my guide. It took several classes before they began to speak with more spontaneity and fewer reservations. It was important that they learned how to talk about it since knowledge and awareness help strengthen our resolve regarding racial equality. In order to resist peer pressure and society's norms a person must know a great deal about racism to begin with.

WORKBOOK WRITING 4-a

1. What does white privilege mean to you?

2. Describe a time in your past when your whiteness seemed to be important to someone in a position of authority.

3. How would your life be different if whiteness became irrelevant? What would you lose? What would you gain?

WORKBOOK WRITING 4-b

What's in a word? Fill in your brief definition of the following words and phrases:

Blackmail _____

Nightmare _____

Black cat _____

Black sheep _____

Black flag _____

Blackguard _____

Black listed _____

Blackout _____

White-collar worker _____

White elephant _____

White fish _____

White flag _____

Whitewash _____

Whiteout _____

We viewed films and read texts about the history of racism in the United States. These were useful, but the most valuable assignments were the more proactive. In one, I asked the students to go into an integrated environment where there were a significant number of people of color and simply observe their experience. They answered questions beforehand and wrote in their journals after. You'll soon have the chance to do the same.

One of the students of color smiled about this exercise. Her name was Jackie. Jackie said she would not have much to write because she believed that no matter where she went everyone would separate themselves automatically: "Whites with whites and blacks with blacks." But on the whole there was a lot of enthusiasm for this exercise from the students of color, who were convinced that it was a good way for the white students to see what the students of color came up against whenever they went into integrated environments. Which is to say, nearly every class every day.

Taking responsibility for white privilege - some things to think about

- ❦ It would be nice if our actions were not representing any person or group, but as you get involved you will be representing racism, the pros and cons of it, wherever you go.

- ❦ It would also be nice if our actions were not challenging anyone else's. It wouldn't be real, but it would be nice.

- ❦ It would be nice if one's seeking inclusion with others of a different ethnicity did not invite the rejection of so many white people who imply you are inadequate. It would also be nice if white people's role models did not conflict with the vision of equality you have in mind for yourself. But of course, that is the implication of the vision you carry.

- ❦ When we integrate, are we doing other cultures a favor? Hardly. Can we be taken advantage of? Definitely. If you get caught up in becoming a representative of whiteness and all that it could be, you become a caricature of yourself, a stereotype. People of color know what is real and what is not. They have been aware of white people for centuries.

❦ When you integrate as part of a process of finding out more about others and yourself (the self that has not become submerged in whiteness through its prejudices), it will be obvious to others that you are working the racial quality muscle.

ASSIGNMENT - BEFORE

Choose an integrated place or event to visit. There should be a significant number of people of color there. Before you go, write answers to these questions:

1. What do you expect to see and feel?

2. How do you expect to be treated?

3. What other expectations do you have?

4. Describe any insecurities or worries you're feeling.

5. Describe any hopes you hold.

ASSIGNMENT - AFTER

While you're involved with your integrated outing, pay attention to details that have anything to do with race and racism. Afterward, write about your experiences.

1. Which of your expectations were met? Which were not? For example: Did everyone get along? Was there any racism? Were you self-conscious if you, as a white person, were in the minority? If you are of color did you notice that other students of color tended to stay together? Were the interactions among most of those present inclusive?

2. Did any of your insecurities or worries prove warranted?

3. Were any hopes realized?

Talking About Race

WRITING INTERVAL

Even when white people seem okay about prejudice they raise
their voice when they speak to me. I am black;
I am not hard of hearing. And it happens at bus stops,
in stores and in class. This makes me wonder
how deep this problem really does go.

Since we have been able to betray others on a daily basis about racism and we have also been misled about it in our own lives there is a lot to consider while doing this work. The need for reflection is great because no matter your standpoint on these issues, racism costs. In this writing interval you will focus on questions that lead into reflection and give you a clearer sense of yourself in the context of your own race story.

You can use these questions in any setting, whether you are working independently or as part of a group. As you read them you will find they cover a lot of ground. That is my intention. They may appear to be in a random order, but they are not. Take breaks when you need to, but try to work through them in order.

1. Can people of color avoid being subjected to racism?

2. Do you believe anyone of color can prevent being affected by racist norms in this culture?

3. If you were of person of color, how do you suppose racism would affect you?

4. With respect to your own color, would you say you were born lucky?

5. Do your relationships depend upon invisibility to keep them going?

6. If you do not pay attention to the color of my eyes, does that mean we are more alike than we might otherwise be? If not, why not?

7. How does this affect your relationship to other white people when you talk about me? If it is too uncomfortable to see me as I am, what kind of relationship do we have?

8. Does being white mean you have it made?

9. Do you think white people have no problems?

10. If you are a person of color, do you believe white people owe you something?

11. I would have to draw the line with (name an ethnic group) when it come to marriage because…

12. An assumption drawn by others about me racially is…

13. Institutionalized racism reinforces…

14. Having a contact sheet of activists would be…

15. Let's pretend you have brown eyes. Do you want that fact to be completely unimportant or overlooked in your relationships?

16. Would this mean that I do not want to see you for who you are?

17. Is that what you want?

18. Does mentioning you "don't care about color" imply you are not a racist?

19. When we see the difference in color among us, why would that suggest we are racist?

20. In order to correct a racist situation I would need…

21. I wish I was lighter because…

22. I imagine that being biracial might be difficult because …but it may also have its advantages. One of those advantages might be…

23. I am white. I would have rather been born…

24. Do we miss anything when we assume oppression is only experienced by black people and that all black people interpret their oppression in the same way?

25. If you believe we don't why do you believe that?

26. If you believe we do, then what do you believe we miss out on?

27. Are there distinctions to be made about racial oppression just as there are about gender and class oppression?

28. Have you ever seen a film with an all-black cast?

29. Do you dissect and analyze black films with an all-black cast as you do films with an all-white cast?

30. If your answer to that question is "no," then why not?

31. Why are most sit-coms white?

32. If you don't like that most sit-coms are white, what can you do about it?

33. Can you do whatever your solution to question #20 was today?

34. How does it change your point of view when you approach an analysis of black women in film, literature and the media and make race first in importance? Second in importance?

35. If you overlook the absence of multiculturalism in the media, does it reduce the impact of diversity in your life today?

36. How does this affect your relationship to other white people when you talk about me?

37. If it is too uncomfortable to see me as I am, what kind of relationship do we have?

38. How would the knowledge we believe we have of one another change today?

39. Why do you think acknowledging someone because of her/his color is wrong?

40. Let's assume you do consider that a problem, what is the remedy for it?

41. As you discover the omission of knowledge about the history of European white people and such greats as Ida B. Wells and W.E.B. DuBois how does it make you feel about your own education so far?

42. Do you lean toward feelings of ignorance, shame or anger; or betrayal?

43. Do you feel protective, depressed, apathetic or overwhelmed?

44. Do the men or women in your life tend to affirm your intelligence or discredit it?

45. Do you feel your self-esteem is diminished in the presence of a man or a woman?

46. Now answer the above question but add color to it. (That is, do you feel your self esteem is diminished in the presence of a man of color, a woman of color? In the presence of a white man, a white woman?)

47. If you were to create a film telling the story of your life so far would it be an action film, documentary, comedy or tragedy?

48. Why?

49. What difference would the style you chose make when compared to other films?

50. Whom do you imagine would be most interested in viewing it and why?

51. Is the audience culturally diverse?

52. If it is, why does the film appeal to a culturally diverse audience? If it does not, then why doesn't it?

CHAPTER FIVE

A NEW IDENTITY

*Racism doesn't give me what I want
without taking something
away from me.*

At the start of the course, just as you may have felt at the start of the book, my students feared that racism was just too big a topic, too thorny a problem for them to handle. But not far into it they began to be aware of real change in themselves and in each other. As these quotes from their journals show, their awareness of themselves and the problem of racism in their lives was growing.

> My position in this culture due to racism may be temporary because it is dependent upon racism in order to continue.

> The entitlement I was raised with has confused me about my self-worth.

> I have no idea how blacks (and I don't mean one homogenized group) interpret my behavior. It could be that it occupies less space in their mind than it does in mine.

> Can a white person survive without group dynamics validating their superiority and protecting them?

> The ironic thing is that the first day of class, I expected
> you (the teacher) to be black....When I thought of race
> I saw only people of color before the class began. When
> I saw my dad's response [to the fact that the teacher was
> white] I realized I do not think that way anymore. I see
> white people as a part of race, at least the race problem.
> This is a big change in my thinking and I am so happy I
> see it that way now.

The students had begun to cope with the subject and the introspection required of them. They clearly felt less apprehensive about talking about racism. Their commitment to doing the work was increasing, and they were motivated by a deep curiosity that I found inspiring.

In race work we want to change the conditions that have contributed to our ignorance and our privilege. The introspection we undergo as we review our histories and reassess the role racism plays in our lives helps us come to a greater understanding of ourselves. This understanding leads us to a transformation — deep change. When we change we are more able to become a catalyst for change. And the best place to start is with the people closest to us.

We all know at least one person who is a racist

If I asked you to, you could name one person who is a racist. From now on you will begin to question their motives. You may even begin to question their intelligence and their humanity. These people are your sisters, your brothers and friends, your mothers and fathers and so many others who are closely involved in your life. They are there at all the key moments of your life — loving, proud, caring. And racist.

How does their racism affect you? How do you feel now about your past reactions to their racism? How will you react tomorrow, next month, in a decade? One of the students, call her Marie, shared an experience she went through with one of the racists in her life — her father.

Marie's prom

All through high school, Marie enjoyed a close friendship with her classmate David, who was African American. Neither of them had been dating, and as the time for the senior prom approached they decided to go together. They were sure to have a good time. The more they talked about the idea the more they liked it. Marie's father, however, did not like it. He surprised Marie by forbidding her to go to the prom with David.

Never before had her father taken much notice of her friendship with David. It was the prom setting, and the possibility of romance, that brought out his anger. Marie was shocked to discover that her father was a racist.

Four years later, in class, Marie was still deeply troubled by her father's reaction, and her own. She not only gave in to her father but she failed to tell her friend David the truth. She was still afraid to tell him, worrying it might hurt him. If she had it to do over, she wrote, she would not have given in to her father. She cared for him, did not want to hurt him, but she would have stood up to him. Or if she'd been forced somehow to give in, she would certainly have told David what had happened.

Secrecy and baggage

I responded to Marie's entry like this:

> You mentioned your friend and the invitation to his prom. You said "no" so you wouldn't have to deal with your dad. You also withheld the truth from your friend about why you would not go. You also feel sad about it. It has been a few years since this happened and it is still bothering you.
>
> I am going to be frank about how I see this because it is such a prime example of some serious manipulations, which I attribute to the recurring love affair white people have with racism in general and how it serves them.

Of course you can completely disagree with me. But I see a lot of secrecy and fear in this situation, and the baggage we carry stays with us for life. It also interferes with our ability to resist racism.

Why did you avoid your dad? It seems to me there are many reasons why you did not approach your dad with this invitation from your black male friend. It was not only because your dad is a "jerk" as you put it, just as it is not simply because he is a racist. Since racism is a compilation of layers of **accumulated prejudices** and judgments, here are a few of the layers I read into the incident:

> I know dad will give me flak, anger, rejection or even some form of punishment, will insult or dismiss me altogether which will offend me and could make me feel like I am less than he is.
>
> If dad acts out in a way that really pushes my buttons about my beliefs I will then have to explain, defend, rebel, move away or retaliate against him.
>
> If I am luckier or more privileged than my black friend, my dad knows that and must believe it is fine. And I know it even if I do not believe it is fine. I like being perceived as better, more innocent and of more value. It reassures me I can get what I want out of life. It is all I have ever known, so why should I speak up and challenge it? If I do I am only hurting myself, right?

After-effects of the prom

If Marie's father had control over the direction and outcome of the friendship, then David's input was ineffectual from the start, wasn't it? Therein lies the danger of racism: it reinforces powerlessness, reducing the effect Marie's friend had in a relationship of his choosing. In a tragic way, he is not completely "in" the relationship. Only a portion of him is, and it is that portion that Marie had control over because she was not being completely honest with him. He might think racism was not an issue. He might think he was perceived as a whole, viable person in her eyes. And because nothing was been said about her father interfering, he remained unaware of this conflict.

If the situation were reversed, would Marie have preferred to be unaware of the real problem? Would you?

The father's rejection of Marie's friend was due to the friend's skin color, plain and simple. And he expected her to honor his prejudice by accepting his authority and power over her and her friend. But there is more to it than that. If Marie rejected her friend and the relationship ended, would she then engage selectively in white-only relationships that wouldn't draw attention from her father? In order to regain some privacy, this might seem a worthwhile compromise. However, Marie would then be choosing whiteness over blackness and, as a result, would probably expect less of herself and of others. For the rest of her life.

WORKBOOK WRITING 5-a

1. What is your opinion of Marie's situation and choices?

2. Write one question each for Marie, her friend David, and Marie's father. Try to come up with questions that help them grow together without anyone being a victim.

The nugget of racism Marie had a chance to examine and bring to the surface will require more attention from her and her father. It can alter their relationships to each other. Without that attention, this relationship is stuck in what could have been. In a way, her father's will enters into her future relationships because she kept his prejudice alive and unchallenged; the residue of unresolved tension may follow her wherever she goes.

If Marie had told David what was going on, then her father's superiority could have been challenged by David and others. Marie may not have known that at the time but her father probably did. Racism was, and is, one of the few ways he has to demonstrate control over her.

Control reassures racists about their worth. The need for it and dependence on it is one of the main roadblocks on the road to racial equality. More about that later on in the chapter.

My comments to Marie continued:

> Since your father handed you this opposition consciously or unconsciously after years of living with him, you and your dad now keep up your relationship at the expense of your self-respect and this young man's self-respect. How much do you respect your friend if you conceal such vital information from him for so long? The fact that it has continued to bother you may be an indication that you do respect him because you feel responsible and it is bugging you. But the respect is hidden under the layers of fear created by aligning yourself with your dad's racism. Racism always costs, however deeply it may be hidden under insecurities about one's self-worth and self-respect. It's tied up in your inheritance. Do you have what it takes to truly respect someone of another color when your father does not? Can you take the emphasis off of that person as a scapegoat for your own issues and your dad's as well?

I also told her that I do not know the answers to those questions but that she may be able to answer them herself.

Racial maturity

Confronting racism requires that we move beyond our adolescence. In race relations we continually seem to fear the responsibilities and strains of adulthood. We need autonomy and maturity where these crucial matters are concerned. Where racism is concerned we are too often like children hoping things will somehow turn out better, as if it is not up to us to learn the language or walk the walk that will dismantle inequality once and for all. But that is not the case today and it will not be the case tomorrow. You will make the difference that will be made. The only hope we can experience is the hope you bring to others and to yourself.

We have the answers to our questions. No one else does. We are responsible for what we already know. No one else is. If you decide to look for an apartment or buy a house you set about finding the information you need. You read, surf the web, ask experts, talk to more experienced friends about how they found an apartment or bought a house. You may even take a class. Likewise, when you're looking for a job or planning to go to a school you find out what you need to know. When we rely upon public assistance for any benefit, we find out what we need to know. Businesses who know racism exists in the work-place do nothing about it. But when they incur the slightest loss in their profits you can be sure they call in an accountant, brainstorm among staff and fix the problem.

As a white person, I have noticed white people put more effort into knowing how to cook than in knowing how deeply impacted by racial injustice people are. I find this deeply disturbing. There is no lack of exposure to racial violence in our neighborhoods, on TV, the Internet and radio. We have not been deprived of the history of civil rights; it is accessible to us.

Racial equality requires personal growth. As mentioned earlier, our sense of hopelessness is an indicator that we must build our racial equality muscle. Our children of all ages deserve to be enabled, to feel hopeful about racial equality, and to be spared the work you are doing today. Many of us know this already yet we still struggle with it. We still give up and give in to racism.

Prepare to be seen differently by your peers

People engaged in race work depart from what has been expected of them or hoped for by others in their lives. You will be considered rebellious or defiant when, in reality, you are simply becoming aware of yourself and what you do not want to be a part of. You find the assertion of your own values both exhilarating and liberating. The new identity feels good.

Some white people, however, will see your involvement in other cultures as a rejection of your own. They realize you are putting yourself at risk when you integrate. They know that your life will involve danger, because when you cross the color line, you enter a **racial danger zone** that was intended for people of color. And yet you do cross.

A new identity means letting go of some things

"I refuse to give up parts of myself," wrote one student early in the course, and from another, "There is so much I'd never give up."

If we are no longer the designated winners, then we are losers. How can we be losers when we have already deemed people of color the losers? And yet racial equality means equal opportunity, so we certainly will incur some losses. Our assumptions of privilege and normalcy will be among the first things to go. We all know that. But we must let go of racism because it is our choice. It is up to us.

In class, the students showed me that there were three pieces of knowledge about themselves that were key in their understanding whiteness and racism:

1. The changes we seek include bringing our unresolved conflicts to the table, resolving and letting them go.

2, A change may come because we willingly dissolve our attachment to the values or traditions that got us here.

WORKBOOK WRITING 5-b

1. Is it necessary to surrender your identity in order to support integration and racial equality?

2. Have you ever feared someone because of his or her color?

3. Have you been fearful of anyone because of your color?

4. What can you do about that fear today?

5. Should a white person resent hearing about the race problem in America?

3. This change will take place due to the knowledge we gain of one another going through a core and irreversible transformation.

I have often wondered if we are too afraid to change; too eccentric to surrender; too cowardly to dissolve our narcissistic ways and too vain to accept maturity and cooperation as a way of life inclusive of all.

Those are tough words for a tough problem. But in the students' writing, I came upon many a line that inferred these very concerns. The pain regarding values could not be overlooked. The concerns they had about losing are clear as they wondered what kind of certainty or security would replace it.

When we lose, we want some assurance that the loss will be replaced with something of more value. But if we lose relationships because we want racial equality, they cannot be replaced. If we lose a job because of our desire for racial equality, we lose the job. We remain attached to our privilege and wonder how things can work out for us when we begin to let go of it.

Wrote one student, "I struggle to fill up my life by my own efforts with things no matter the cost." This student was concerned that his struggle might be feeding racism. He was convinced he had gained his drive and his position independent of anyone else. But he did not. His accomplishment, his assertion of worth, independence and competition existed on the foundation of white supremacy. His success had ensured another's defeat.

We often feel the need to "hold on" to ideas, plans, guilt, inabilities, and even our conflicted identities about race. The students were stressed out, not hopeful. Again the strains of fear, competition and loss seemed to coincide with their confusion as they tried to figure out their relationship to racism. That may also be true of you.

At this point in the book, the prospects for racial equality may seem rather poor. Who are you competing against right now? Is this competition feeding your desire for racial equality or does it diminish it?

The new identity and the victim-oppressor pattern

The legacy of **chattel slavery** in this country casts a foreboding shroud across the descendants of enslaved people as well as the descendants of enslavers. It also affects those who came to this country later to build their lives upon the foundation of wealth created by slavery. It is part of our identity and we must dissect this legacy if we are to truly change. Unfortunately, part of the legacy is that when people of color hold white people accountable, when they are impatient or unfriendly, white people can simply drop the issue as if it had never surfaced. We can hide behind the defenses discussed in chapter three. Our role is mutable. Like actors, we have the power to mask our true position on racial equality.

But the reality, whether we face it or not, is that the legacy of slavery has delayed our development. It has put us on hold. I am not sure how much we can know about ourselves without gaining more knowledge of slavery and the impact it still has on us today. That impact can perhaps best be seen in the roles white people tend to fall into when interacting with people of color. These roles mirror, and keep alive, the victim-oppressor pattern established during slavery.

The issue of domestic abuse tends to attract a good deal of attention. People seem to care about it and many feel free to analyze the psychodynamics between the abuser and the abused. But they seem less interested in a similar dynamic when it comes to racism and the impact slavery had and continues to have on our own psyches and actions.

What happens next? Equality opens doors

After the abuse pattern is dissolved, there may remain such a residue of pain that the parties choose not to communicate with one another. But if communication is seen as an option, there are now more choices, since both parties stand on equal ground. What might that communication look like?

"What do you want from me?" the abuser (white people) asks of people of color. We want to be able to trust that people of color can accept the fact that we have changed. We also want to be assured that people of color will not hold us responsible for past offences.

That may not be possible. It will take time for us to crystallize our position and intent in the hopes of securing the most desirable outcome from the admissions we must make of any wrong doing toward people of color. Then maybe they will choose to go through the process of recognition and acceptance of our needs. But maybe they will not. There is loss in forgiveness that they may not care to experience. There is a surrender of anger and resentment when one forgives.

We have no control over the outcome of our efforts. It will be up to people of color to decide what they may want from us, if they want anything at all.

We feel our way into a new identity

Because white people are in the dominant position we can delay asking for forgiveness; we can postpone exhibiting, in word and deed, our desire for equality. But when we are done with delay and postponement, a very fruitful process can begin. This process involves recognition of the oppressive role we have perpetuated, efforts at reconciliation, and acceptance of the importance of feeling, for it is only through emotional work that a new identity can be achieved.

It is not going to be possible to simply think our way into it. Logical conclusions will not be very important. We have been hiding behind logic so much and it has not helped. It is simply not enough.

Not getting discouraged

You are beginning to realize why the very foundation of your soul can seem to crumble beneath your feet when you speak to another white person about racism and white privilege. Now you know why, in a racist situation when racism is not even considered a basis for a problem, you may, as chapter three describes it, freeze. You do not pause. You freeze. And by now you have felt that very painful descent into the abyss of caring about racism.

Now you understand what happens to white people when they come to recognize racism because you have come to recognize racism and will continue to. But this time you will see how and why you do and that there is more to it than acknowledging that it exists or claiming to care about it. It is like walking through one door and finding another open and then another and another. These are open doors to a new identity. From the new identity, you see the advantages of caring about this problem and the changes that will come because you care.

As we have said, fears, doubts and delays are not left behind, nor is discouragement. In fact, it's natural to become discouraged along the way. Some causes for discouragement are:

- The people in our history books are our relatives.
- We have to question the true motives of our ancestors without actually knowing them.
- We have to question the silence of our immediate families about the Civil Rights Movement.
- Real change takes forever.

White people tend to give up on each other too easily when the issue is race. We let each other off the hook because the result of our queries and the analysis necessary to make any progress at all requires change and we know that it does. So it takes strength to resist shutting down when this exploration becomes difficult. We are all in a box of oppression, but not for the same reasons and never with the same outcome as people of color.

It's also easy to become discouraged because so far there is no happy ending to work for or look forward to. There is no immediate gratification. But there is an on-going satisfaction that we have tackled a problem many don't want any part of. There is also an obligation to disassemble the mechanism that keeps us more neutral than we may want to be on this subject. In the next chapter, you will see how a young man named Roger wrestled with his white privilege and began to walk the walk that called for change through self-awareness.

WORKBOOK WRITING 5-c

1. If you woke up this morning and there had been no racism in your life, how would your life have been different?

2. What would you recommend to help heal the problems we have mentioned in this book?

3. Whose help would you need in order to start working on racial equality in your own life?

4. What organization would you call up today to become more racially integrated in your community?

5. What does white privilege mean to you today?

CHAPTER SIX

WHAT FREEDOM AWAITS US

*While people of color live with racism and it defines them,
whiteness defines whites and we are also living within
that which defines us ... we'll need to unravel ourselves
from it and yet we may not be freer if we do.
Yet there is a possibility that we may be.
It seems to me we deserve to find out
what freedom awaits us if we do.*

In moments when you attempt to get involved in racial equality, you will become exhilarated and validated. The power struggles you have observed are now more personal, more accessible. Change is something you can participate in if you haven't already. There is joy in knowing you can care deeply about this problem. There are steps that will make a difference and every step counts. Your observations matter!

We are no longer in denial about racism. We are no longer convinced that our role in it is hopeless or ineffectual. The freedom found in developing our abilities to encourage racial equality increases our desire to see and to know more. This freedom can be found at home, in school, in business and in churches. When you do not stay within the designated white-on-white relationships box you've been put in, when white privilege no longer defines you, and you can identify yet still refuse to be owned by racism, you are free.

Some of my students experienced this freedom during the course. Here is one account:

> This last weekend, an old co-worker was down for the weekend, and she, two current co-workers and I all went out. One of them is African American. Her name is Ann. Ann had just graduated from college. We are pretty good friends, we write to each other and I recently went to Maryland to see her. My first realization was that we had a genuine friendship. The thing I was wishing for I actually had, although in my previous journal entry I had written that I thought only my brother had good friendships with men of color. Anyway, we went out and danced at a night club. We had so much fun! We were on equal terms; it wasn't different than hanging out with anyone else. Except that I'm in awe of my friend, not because she is black but because she's beautiful, intelligent and super-cool.
>
> Then we split-up for the evening. My two black friends went to their school and my other friend and I went to a party. At the party were two black men I knew and I realized they are at most of the parties I go to. I have also had them over to my place a few times during the summer. And again I realized I have African American friends and it is natural. I know this isn't a big revelation; it was just comforting to know that it isn't weird.

Racism is what's weird, white privilege is weird. When we start to see just how weird they are we're starting to glimpse a world that's free of them.

DWBW: Driving while black and white

Roger, a white student in class, was in a car with his African American friend William. William was driving. A cop pulled them over. He began to interrogate William, leaving Roger out of it. Roger was shocked that the clichéd DWB (driving while black) experience was happening right before his eyes. As his friend was questioned roughly, searched and humiliated Roger could do nothing but sit quietly with his anger and hurt. Both he and William remained uncharacteristically passive, sensing that their safety and freedom depended on it.

By the time Roger discussed this **DWBW** experience with the class, he had many mixed emotions to process. It opened his eyes to the perversion of white power within a racist context. Had Roger shown his anger to the officer, or interfered at all, his friend would have gotten even worse treatment. Although Roger never quite believed that before, he understood it now. Roger had no real knowledge or interest in the politics that controlled their lives until this had happened. He knew his presence had altered the outcome of a fundamental injustice perpetrated upon his friend.

Same car same cop, two very different experiences

William said he was afraid. Roger had seen and felt William's fear and had been afraid for him. But while William experienced fear, Roger was simply startled. While William experienced humiliation, Roger experienced alarm. While William experienced relief when he was told he could go, Roger experienced anger.

There is a difference between the two and that difference contributed to shaping the relationship between these two men. In one instant, Roger became the caretaker while William was in need of care. This may not be what they were looking for in their relationship to one another, and yet this is what was imposed upon them. This is one of the consequences of racism. There are three entities in this relationship now: William, Roger and racism.

The likelihood of a white male bringing up an incident of this kind to the group is greater than that of the male of color. Why? The white officer had protected the white male. The white officer had no conscious interest in Roger. So Roger was distanced from the violence exacted upon William by the invasion of privacy. Roger's presence made him something of a hero, whether that is what he wanted or not. It may have protected William from more harassment. Although Roger could observe, sense and witness the lack of control he had, he could still remain safe. A dispassionate perspective is what he was left with no matter how much he cared about his friend. Like the cop, he was in the power position. But it was a position he had nothing to do with, did not ask for, and may not have realized he could benefit from were it not for this experience with William.

Had William been with another man of color, the incident may have been prolonged and who knows what else he may have had to endure.

Instead, Roger's whiteness may have discouraged the cop from going any further. It was enough for the cop to impose white

WORKBOOK WRITING 6-a

1. How do you feel about William?

2. How do you feel about the police in this situation?

3. Is experiencing shame about racism inevitable?

4. Do you think it is important for families of color to discuss racism?

5. What do you think about Roger and his position in this situation?

male dominance on William and expose it to Roger. Roger was aware of the role racism played in this incident.

Let's review the process each male goes through based on my rendition and interpretation of events. We'll put their reactions into two separate columns to see which range of experience you might prefer if you were one of the two men. Circle what you believe to be the most probable choices:

William	Roger
Fear	Startled
Humiliation	Alarm
Relief	Anger
Blasé	Sympathetic

We will take this a step further with a few more questions for reflection.

WORKBOOK WRITING 6-b

1. Which of the two men would you want to be? Why?

2. If you observed a person of color being pulled over on the road by an officer, what would be your first assumption about it?

WORKBOOK WRITING 6-b

3. There was a moment of the transition from friend (Roger) to caretaker. One result of racism was that Roger and William took new roles imposed upon them by an incident. How would you expect that to affect their relationship?

4. Given the circumstances, whom do you imagine speaks up first about what just happened, William or Roger? Assuming they do talk about what just happened, who might apologize to whom for what happened to both of them?

5. Would William still want to keep the friendship with Roger? If so, does he lose anything in the process? If you answered "yes," what does he lose?

6. Does Roger let his friend know what it felt like to be responsible for protecting him?

WORKBOOK WRITING 6-b

7. Do you have any further thoughts on the subject regarding either man independent of one another?

8. Do you see William and Roger as equals now? If so, why? If not, why not?

This is one isolated incident. Multiply that incident by many more in William's life and you get an idea of the impact it has on his point of view about himself and the world in which he lives. Now imagine the stress he must live with from day to day.

It is tragic that some need to wait so long before they understand the gaps between people of color and white people in what we might consider normal situations. If children and adolescents were presented with the truth of it before they reached college, they would be better prepared to make decisions that can dissolve their complicity before it begins.

White men can disavow their privilege

Perhaps Roger by now has become a white man who disavows his privilege. I have known more than a handful of white men who have gone through ideological contortions in order to stand for racial equality and discard their entitlement in many areas. Some were educated but refused to raise their status because they resisted increasing their power. Others refused to own real estate or may not have had children in order to prevent themselves from assuming roles of authority over others. The role authority plays in racism has been more than enough for them to live with already.

Everyone has their own way of coping with their knowledge of racism. We each have ways of taking action that others may not be aware of. But there are inevitable stages of maturation from the naïve individual to the empowered individual. The element of protection in white culture combined with the naiveté we are often raised with has created a tidal wave of differences between us and people of color. The effects of those differences are as staggering as they are complex. Both discourse and action create opportunities for change, and there cannot be one without the other.

White women often confuse racism with sexism

White women often compare sexism to a person of color's issues of racial inequality in our society. Therefore barriers to a mutual understanding of each other's dilemma would be inevitable. It is hard for white women to put their issues aside; somehow or other they simply must inject a portion of their own experience into the experience of women of color as they imagine that experience to be. But we imagine the experience of women of color according to our own life experience. It is futile to do so. I don't really know why we try. I believe it is enough to listen to women of color knowing what they tell us about their own experience of us without needing to inject ourselves into their experience at all.

But white women get offended if not stunned when they are asked to keep their experience, which can only be within the context of their whiteness, separate. If they are working on these issues at all progress can and will take place. But only by being who we really are.

Once I was asked why black women get so impatient with white women about racism and I thought, How patient can one be with one's own oppressor? Our roles have never been reversed, nor healed. They have not entirely dissolved. We are living with the residue of slavery between us. We are living with racial inequality. No matter our effort or our intention, people of color can speak for themselves. We are not a part of the experience of being of color. We live in a society that continues to infuse white people with a power that takes away from the power of people of color.

Where are we now

"When we talk about race," one student wrote, "I try to convince myself that there isn't that much to say and then I realize how much there really is."

You have come a long way since you opened this book. You probably realize now, as did this student, how very much there really is to talk about. You have examined your childhood, reassessed influences in your upbringing and considered the very active relationship between racism and violence. You have also reflected on the role that so-called innocence plays in white privilege and discovered strengths you already may have or will need to develop regarding this work.

Because we are learning how to integrate our interest in racial equality into our lives this journey will take you a step further so you can begin to use what you know. There are many ways to work the racial equality muscle but at each point in our work self-reflection continues to matter. We can never escape our whiteness as we grow through this process. Hopefully we will not want to. Hopefully we will simply continue to change what it represents to others and to ourselves through our actions.

Action requires working the racial equality muscle and that can take time and many steps until we get it right. You may stumble and fall but clumsiness and humiliation are not really the most important consequences of your development. Mistakes happen. What is most important is the risk you take, the growth you demand of yourself and the assertion of your perspective and ideals.

Here are seven beginning steps we can take

1. Listen to others and respond when the issue is race or racism.

2. Accept the fact that the drama of our own lives is equal to the drama of the lives of others.

3. Refuse to remain passive even when others believe passivity is a solution to any situation that involves racism.

4. Realize that our way of coping with racism or resisting racism may be different from someone else's.

5. Refuse to protect other white people from what we consider racism to be.

6. When there is racial tension on the job, at school, in a dorm or anywhere else, draw attention to it.

7. Inform our educators, social service professionals and others in our community about our interest in racial equality and ask them what they are doing about it in their professions.

Write about it

I'd like you to do some freestyle writing – not questions this time, just whatever comes up.

Write about what's going on racially in your own backyard, where you work, where you shop, where you get your hair done. Why have you chosen the job that you have? Why do you go to that particular salon? Or, a particular grocery store? How integrated is it? What kind of activity goes on about race in these places? Are you comfortable? Are you demonstrating your desire for racial equality there? Do conversations ever take place that upset you about race? If so then what is going on? If not, how can that be?

You have places to go, people to see already. You can try it today. Now get writing!

Others will question your motives

As you work for the freedom you know awaits you and become more clear about your motives, you will find that others continue to question them. Here are some of the questions you will probably be asked:

- 🍎 Are you in pursuit of your own ideals to facilitate equality?
- 🍎 If so, are you using people of color and possibly being a racist doing that?
- 🍎 Are you trying to find out what is missing in your own upbringing?
- 🍎 Why can't you stay within your own racial group even though you have formed such strong opinions about racism?
- 🍎 Is your freedom dependent upon being included in other cultures?
- 🍎 If so, doesn't that make you especially vulnerable?

Consider anything anyone suggests. It may or may not apply. Just remember that people of color and white people bring their own prejudices to you and you'll need to decide what you are doing and why you are doing it for yourself. Evidence of failure in your efforts can be what people are hoping for. After all racial equality would change everything and many people have found their nook, their way of coping. They do not want to change.

When we're silent and passive we lose an opportunity

Silence only feeds racism. A lack of action is a lost opportunity. Even when we do act we may wonder later, as did the student below, if we could have done more.

At a popular doughnut store, my friends and I stopped for coffee. We sat at the counter talking with other restaurant regulars. A yellowish-beige car pulled up and several people commented on how ugly the car was. The driver, a black man, gets out of the car and the waitress says, "Leave it to a spook to drive a car like that." The regulars laughed and started discussing what other color cars "those" people drive. I couldn't believe my ears!

I was absolutely outraged. I said, "Excuse me?" out loud and everyone just gave me a funny look. I then said to my friends "Are we ready to go?" And started to go. They followed. Even though I said something and we left I did not feel like that was enough. In part that is why I am in this class right now. There has to be more I can do.

We have covered the reasons why we want to stay silent in situations like this one at the doughnut store. We understand rejection. We understand loss. We also understand that people in our lives are threatened by threats to their racism. Many equate the end of racism with having less for themselves, or with becoming the "losers" in the competition they see as life. Others resist having to learn more about it and accept the inclusion of other cultural norms in their life.

We all know this already. We also know this complicates our own position on racism from time to time. Others may be unwilling to be subjected to the fear, alienation, abandonment, betrayals, isolation, punishment and rejection we know will follow our assertion of racial equality at home, at work, while socializing. It is no wonder racism has not really been dealt with or healed yet in this country. With so many anxieties and insecurities about it we do not know how to identify or assimilate our feelings about racism. Hence we remain silent, or don't act with as much integrity as we wish we could.

Being willing to undergo a process of understanding racism and its impact on our culture is courageous. But without understanding ourselves first our effort to disengage from racist norms will be somewhat useless, for when we are challenged we won't be able to deal with those challenges — unless we have undergone some introspection beforehand. Here is another chance for that introspection. As always, save your work. It's important.

WORKBOOK WRITING 6-c

1. My child is protected from racism because...

2. The expectations of bi-racial children are different than that of white children and children of two parents of color because...

3. It is not unusual to see white people mask their racism behind friends, lovers, and co-workers. If white people are not responsible and there is nothing they can do about racism, then why does masking it become necessary?

4. Is experiencing shame about racism inevitable?

WORKBOOK WRITING 6-c

5. What does white privilege mean to you?

6. White people can accumulate prejudices without ever being held accountable for them. Where do you suppose white people's ambivalence about racism stems from?

CHAPTER SEVEN

VALIDATION FOR YOUR EFFORTS

When I talk to my friends of color about racism and how much it
upsets me, I don't get a compassionate response. I simply don't.....
If I rely on white friends for empathy, they really can't give it;
they are very defensive or callous. I get more support
in class for these struggles of conscience
with racism. I would not have expected
to get more help in a classroom
among strangers than with friends
but that is the way it is.

As you work for racial equality, expect to create change.
Don't stop until you get enough! But do slow down along the
way to appreciate what you are doing. And do the same for
other white people.

Daniel, a student of color in class, told one of the white students that she shouldn't look for approval from people of color all
the time, "'cause she won't get it." Alice said she had often looked
at blacks in particular and would smile at them. "I try to acknowledge blacks in the street and elsewhere to show a kind of solidarity to them. To show that I am not a racist." Daniel laughed and said,
"You can't really think we need your approval?" He also told her
that when they think of white people, they do it more selectively.

And "Sometimes when they are out walking they are not thinking of white people at all — they are simply out walking."

Alice came to understand her need for approval from people of color and to realize that they did not have the same need. She also understood that she had been very alone in her consciousness of and interest in racism. She wanted to remedy that. She didn't believe she needed to be so isolated and she was right. She took my class and that is what my course was for - anyone who felt they were too caring, too sensitive, too angry, too frustrated, too alone to cope with the isolation racism imposes upon us.

You must find ways to approve of your own need to process racism. It takes time. We all need that. You might find this validation in books, films, organizations, and a few choice relationships and courses that deal with this subject.

White people often resent the implication that they are not doing anything. Some of the resentment is the result of their own mixed feelings and uncertainty about whether or not racism is really just and if it does in fact protect them. Seek out more knowledge on the subject because knowledge changes you. Learn more. It will help reinforce and validate your position in this work.

Consider what it takes to resist racism and acknowledge your strengths. We build more confidence in ourselves as we address our concerns and develop communication skills that enhance our abilities in both our personal and professional life. We can also inspire others with our fortitude and creativity.

Packing up

Imagine that you wake up at birth to discover you live in the city and you think to yourself:"I wanted to be born in the country." But since you were born in the city, you must remain there until you grow up and can move on your own to the country. Meanwhile, you adapt to your surroundings. You become accustomed to front stoops, and buildings lined up one right next to the other. The steady roar of the subway and traffic begins to sound normal to you. It becomes difficult to imagine life any other way.

You absorb the opinions of those who are perfectly happy in the city. When you talk about country life, people warn you about its dangers, or they just ignore you. Perhaps you even stop talking about wanting to live in the country. And yet you feel restless and discontented. You love the people who raised you, but you also know that in the end the city is not for you. Eventually you do leave.

When you are white and you want racial equality, you will always be restless and discontented with racism. You will wonder, How can people live with racism? And how can I possibly be happy if I must live the same way? You will want to "move to the country," to a place of racial equality.

But here the analogy breaks down. Because those working to solve the problem of racism in their lives eventually understand that a physical move, to an integrated community for example, is not the solution, or not the whole solution anyway. They come to realize that their happiness depends upon **psychic integration**. They grew up in the city and the city's ways are still in them. We grew up in racism and must own it within us before we can truly relocate.

Anyone can be in an integrated environment and still be a racist, but you won't do that. So you have begun to find out how you can go about beating the odds and discovered that it is very difficult to do. Nearly impossible. You see that you need to re-define the position you are in because the position you are in suggests you are superior to people of color.

That realization is not an ending but a beginning. What follows can free you to come to grips with a problem that requires many solutions. To your surprise, a part of the solution is you!

The knowledge of white privilege, the history of psychological and economic strategies incorporated in a white person's upbringing to maintain both status and even racial vanity, have been intentionally shaped to discourage you from dealing with it or realizing your own power. But you were an adolescent. You are mature now. You do have power. You are part of the solution.

The moving truck is here. We're packing the boxes and saying goodbye to the city. Do you feel a sense of accomplishment? You should. Race work is hard work and we've been doing it.

Healing begins with a desire for change

When we consider whiteness in our times, we need to acknowledge that white people have also been betrayed by racism. Wounds get worse over time when they are left untreated; at least the wound is open before us now and we have been examining it. Perhaps it is even more obvious to us than it was before and we are better prepared to treat it. That means that now you can do something about it.

Let's return to the child we left behind for a moment and take a look at what has happened to her:

The child woke up in a family that was unaware of how harmful city life was to their child. It did not make them unhappy enough to learn more about it. They understood city life. It was all they knew. They thought their child (you) would like it too. They gave her all the benefits city life had to offer. The child did not know enough about the country to express what she wanted to convey to her parents about her need to live in the country. The child kept trying to adapt and looked to others for help but everyone seemed just fine with life in the city.

Racism is like that. Not liking racism is like that. Trying to get support for your dissatisfaction can be a lonely process. Expressing your problems with it may get meager results but only for a time. So you keep going and must find others who care about what you believe is wrong about racism. Then you start to try to fix it. But city life can be just fine. In the analogy, the difference is a matter of preference, like a favorite color. In the reality, racism is toxic, always wrong, never a matter of preference.

Everyone needs to move to the country.

Accept useful analogies along the way

"I am still too white," wrote one student, "to feel strong, valid, honest, real and uninhibited around a black person or a group of black people."

114

I was surprised by this student's expression "still too white." I wonder how many of you have also felt that way? She also wrote that she felt she was on the inside of something recognizing her fears. I think that is a wonderful way to put it, a bit like an embryo in the sac waiting for the right moment to be born. Who is to say it should not be a painful time, disturbing yet compelling? Sorting through racism is worthy of that. When you work on racism you give birth to yourself — the environment you came from was not enough. You do not know why yet but you are still working it all out.

Noelle was a senior when she took my class. Her father and mother visited her on campus for a holiday, having traveled from the Midwest. While they were out for dinner she told them about this course and discussed some of the stories she'd heard in class and all she had been learning about herself, her history and the others in class. She and her family were white. When they finished her father said he was surprised that a course like Let's Talk about Race was being taught in a college. The black professor teaching it, he went on, must be taking quite a risk.

When she told him the teacher was white, he was shocked!

Well, white people are full of surprises. Twenty years ago did I see myself creating a course of this kind and teaching it? No. Twenty years ago I was still hoping that we would not need it.

Your definition of racism and mine

Here is my definition of racism:

> Racism is a systemic psychological and economic approach to life imposed upon the psyche of individuals from infancy onward. Its origins were created out of the myth that white people are superior to people of color. Through slavery and enforced labor it has survived and will continue to survive as long as white privilege remains intact. It can be unlearned just as it has been learned. Racism relies upon ignorance in order to remain effective. It cannot bear to give up power. It loves money, fears poverty and despises sobriety. Racism thrives on all addictions and yet it loathes attachment. It is at once deeply personal while it is wholly incapable of intimacy.

I recognize that this is not a flawless definition. Yet it is the product of my own personal experience with racism. Racism speaks to me. It speaks to me about who you are. Racism speaks to you — it tells you who I am. Racism informs me of my capabilities and limitations while it strips away my capabilities and limitations.

Now it is your turn to define racism

Be sure to refer to it again long after you have finished this book and make note of any changes you want to make. To some extent, your definition of racism will change as you change. That has happened to me.

Be sure you don't compromise yourself to benefit any group while you make up your definition of racism. You have become dependent upon a constant theme of alienation and estrangement. You have suffered a great deal at the hands of white people who are racists. Keep developing the coping skills I referred to in chapter four so when you have aligned yourself with racial equality you can remember what your goal is no matter the cost. Many of us do this every day. We each have our own stories to tell, stories that validate the fears we have had when we knew we were unwilling to be racists. Remember that white supremacy is dependent upon silence and complicity.

Be prepared for conflict

Ann had this to say about her own concerns as she evolved through this work:

> I've been thinking a lot about family, my family and how I will be able to integrate them into my life as I do this work. How do I hold them responsible for whatever share of it is theirs and accept that they will not do the work that is needed of them, and still hold on to them? Well, maybe I can but I must be ready to accept the consequences of being so honest and what it means for our relationship.

Working on racism can give fleeting results. What happens when we sit through the discomfort and displacement because we refuse to surrender to it? Understanding, compassion, anger, resentment or a little of each happen. Will all of the stereotypes which may have informed you of yourself and others dissolve? No, probably not. If they do, what happens next? You happen; just you, you and no racism.

Speak from what you know

Recognize that living a life that disavows your participation in racism may mean that through rejecting inequality as an inevitable part of being white, you are taking responsibility for yourself. By confronting racism you have begun to put yourself forward in life without taking anything away from someone else. This is the nature of resistance in action.

We have earned the right to stand up for ourselves and may have already found that speaking up about our position has consequences. We also may have discovered that our position on racism seems to define our value to other white people. This stage of growth is wrought with alarming twists in our relationships, and although it has been difficult, this juncture is pivotal to our development and includes being willing to enter the racial danger zone.

Before you opened this book you had wondered what could be done about racism. You knew there was so much pain in our lives because of it. You understand that people of color live with a duality of consciousness regarding it because they live in an environment where there can be no trust. They struggle with the fear white supremacist values call for in their lives every day.

Think about it ...

When do you believe a white person should give up their comfort-zones and delve into this subject? What are the signs to watch out for when racist norms become unbearable?

There are four steps we have taken which have already changed us as we have processed racism together:

1. We pursued more knowledge of others and ourselves.

2. We examined our upbringing to see what attitudes about racism we had been persuaded to accept.

3. We began to hold ourselves and others accountable in both words and actions.

4. We walked through the threshold of tolerance into a state of self-assertion.

We have discovered that racism hurts white families and that no person of color can define the truth of white peoples' relationship to racism for white people. No one can determine the impact racism has had on the psychological development of white people within the culture, society, community and family like white people can.

Just how deeply affected white people are by the disclosure and analysis of their role in racism today remains to be seen. What is already obvious, however, is that white people have been and remain profoundly affected by racism; and, racism means we have been included in a betrayal, silence and a wound that has contributed to a split and a division of loyalties between mother and daughter, father and son. Out of this silence, dysfunction within the white family unit thrives. What damages us the most is our unwillingness to change and the deep-rooted delusions of grandeur we hold on to as if our lives depended upon it. For some reason we need to maintain a narcissistic edge over others. Perhaps we fear becoming expendable and if we impose a certain kind of ongoing cruelty on others we can convince ourselves that we are safer, more durable perhaps or even invincible than we really are. But no matter what our views on this subject may be, racism re-creates a bondage to relationships we rely upon for safety and comfort while we remain in an increasing state of anxiety. It seems to me there is enough evidence to prove that complicity comes at a very high price and the ultimate solution to this problem is that we must begin to consider healing whiteness, our past, our present and our future.

Let's review what we know about ourselves

We know we are contradictory. We rely upon freedoms others do not have. We have strained relationships and more neurosis than we can stand. We know our introduction to the world and to others is misleading and there are cracks in the lining of our understanding of ourselves that ensure tragic results.

Why? Because we live in a multicultural world and many of us know that living inside of whiteness has not prepared us for it. We have been sold a bill of goods that is deeply flawed. We have been raised to love and embrace only ourselves so when we move out of the white-box into diversity we are on our own. We become pioneers, rebels or missionaries. We become labels reflecting stereotypes and take on roles we never intended to assume because our desire for integration, coupled with our insistence on having racial equality in our lives, is often misunderstood by others. Racism so permeates our society that we stand out whether we want to or not.

Many white people work on racial equality

The most common knowledge and assumptions about us are threaded into a social construction of race and class but we can and often do deconstruct those assumptions.

When we do accomplish our tasks we become living proof that what we had been warned about becoming is neither awkward nor dangerous. We discover we are not acting out of defiance but out of resolution because the extent to which we can have racial equality in our lives contributes to our welfare rather than diminishing it.

Many of us have a reunion to look forward to when we work through these problems. Many of us will find peace within ourselves when we work through these problems. In doing this work you will find yourself undergoing several changes while you are in transition. While I did, I wrote a testimonial to it that I'd like to share with you now.

> I started out with racism and have ended up with resistance. It is more than I was prepared for and more than I was trained to deal with. It is a vocation. It is also a conscious approach to a way of being in the world because there is no other way.

> If I slip up or make mistakes and need to be quiet in the face of something disturbing, that serves as a reminder that the expectations of myself are not that I go through it well but that I go through it at all.

> When I get tired I read a paper or watch the news, look at a sit-com or walk to the store. I watch race crimes. I witness consumerism. I stare at the stereotypes and remember that today and everyday someone is being killed while I live; someone is being tortured while I get discouraged and someone is being imprisoned while I am free.

> Where racism is concerned all I keep learning is that if I ask the question then I have the answer. If there is no language for whiteness I need to put it into words so there can be a language for it. If there is no psychology that can address white supremacy than I must create a psychology that addresses it. If there is no church or spiritual belief that includes my way of being in the world then I must create one for myself, and wherever this path leads I will continue to follow.

GLOSSARY

Accumulated prejudices - Biases that gradually build up over time

Apathy - A lack of feeling or emotion

Chattel slavery - Moveable property. In this case, African people

Collective guilt - Denoting a group of persons considered a single unit with an awareness of wrong-doing or crimes accompanied by feelings of remorse or shame

Color-blind - Inability to identify something or someone by using colors.

Comfort zone - Condition or degree of comfort

Defenses - Methods of protecting something

Denial - A refusal to acknowledge the existence of something

Disassociate - To disconnect things in your mind

Disclosure - Secret information made public

DWBW - (Driving while black and white) - European white male or female in a car with a driver of color

Fairytale ending - Happing ending based on fantasy

False innocence - An absence of guilt that is not based on the truth

Freeze - To be unable to act, react or speak in a normal way

Guilt - An awareness of wrongdoing

Inclusion - Presence in a group

Institutionalized racism - White supremacy as normal

Learned helplessness - Refusing to take charge

Multiculturalism - Of more than one culture

Narcissistic - Excessive self-admiration and self-centeredness

Psychic integration - Organization of thoughts in the human mind

Quagmire of conflict - An awkward or dangerous conflict

Race story - Your own history within the context of race/ism

Racial danger zone - Entering an area about race that is no longer comfortable

Racial equality - Equality between the races

Racial equality muscle - Developing skills that increase your ability to confront racist assumptions of yourself and others

Racist assumptions - Ideas formed and developed from racist ideas

Stereotype - To repeat without variation

White box - To accept stereotypes about oneself when one is European white, as "normal" and to live within the confines of those assumptions of normalcy even when they are oppressive or against one's own desire for racial equality

White privilege - Benefits in society for being a white person

NOTES

NOTES

NOTES

ABOUT THE AUTHOR

In July of 1951, I was the third of four children born to Dr. & Mrs. George Albert Graham in Brooklyn, N.Y. The name I had been given at birth was Patricia Anne. I attended St. Saviour's Grammar School in Park Slope and Adele's after school program.

In Sept. of 1969 I graduated from St. Agnes Female Seminary for Young Ladies on Avenue R & East 23rd Street in Brooklyn, N.Y. and attended Georgian Court College in Lakewood, N.J. for about 7 months. I left GCC College to experience the freedom and autonomy I needed, deeply impacted by the politics of the time, the Viet Nam war and civil rights movement.

In 1970 I married George Allen Williams, a Viet Nam veteran. We had two children and divorced in 1979. During these years I worked as a waitress, in a teen program for adolescents with disabilities and in politics (The U.S. Peace Council). I had also worked as a singer.

During the 1980's I moved to Montgomery, Al. for a year then returned to NYC to work for the D.C. 1707 Local 205 Welfare Fund on Varick Street. Bits and pieces of my writings were published in journals and magazines and I had "come out," having discovered I was a lesbian during this time period. I was invited to stay at Kate Millett's Art Colony for Women in Poughkeepsie, NY for the summer of 1990 where I worked on her tree farm and on my writing.

In 1991 I moved to Seattle, WA. To celebrate my 40th birthday I changed my name legally to Kaolin, dropping a surname before moving to Massachusetts. I attended Holyoke Community College in 1994 and received certification in early childhood development, then transferred to the University of Massachusetts at Amherst. While at the university I designed and taught a course titled, "Let's

Talk about Race: Confronting Racism through Education" through the independent studies program sponsored by the women's studies department. When I graduated in 2000, I had decided I would write a book about that course and on January 15, 2010 *Talking About Race: A Workbook About White People Fostering Racial Equality in Their Lives* was published by Crandall, Dostie & Douglass Books, Inc.